Greg and Jimmy are investing their lives in transforming a generation. *Small Matters* shows us how we can all make a world-changing difference in the lives of children.

—**Vince Antonucci,** pastor, Verve Church;
author, *God for the Rest of Us*

Jimmy and Greg weave together Scripture, research, and their experience to give you and me a remarkable tool that will change not just us but the kids we care about.

—**Kara Powell,** executive director, Fuller Youth Institute

Greg and Jimmy have impacted hundreds of thousands of kids and families, and now they share powerful insights on how we can make a difference in our own corner of the world.

—**Jud Wilhite,** senior pastor, Central Church; author, *Pursued*

Prepare to have your heart wrecked, your hope renewed, and your vision enlarged. Jimmy and Greg help us think small in order to do something big that matters.

—**Gene Appel,** senior pastor, Eastside Christian Church

These are two of my favorite people writing on a topic so universal no one can disagree, but few have addressed with a fraction of the vigor and impact.

—**Pat Gelsinger,** CEO, Vmware

Small Matters is a brilliant theological blueprint for how adults can train up the next generation to be world-changers of this generation! Read this book!

—**Albert Tate,** lead pastor, Fellowship Monrovia

A must-read for everyone who is serious about seeing extreme poverty eliminated, communities transformed, and an entire generation of young people being given the hope of Jesus.

—**Tim Harlow,** visionary leader, Parkview
Christian Church; author, *Life On Mission*

Small Matters broadens the critical conversation needed to address what prevents today's children from thriving: we must reach those trapped by poverty and those held back by prosperity.

—**David Staal,** president, Kids Hope USA

Greg and Jimmy not only help us to see why we must move kids from the edge to the center of our attention in our homes and churches, they show us how.

—**Ben Cachiaras,** lead pastor, Mountain Christian Church

Greg and Jimmy are what my church calls hope traffickers. Even more, they've perfected a model that is going viral. It's a movement none of us will want to say we missed.

—**Eddie Lowen,** lead pastor, West Side Christian Church

In *Small Matters*, you'll find how faith communities and families can partner to make sure the next generation is known more for its compassion than its consumption.

—**Reggie Joiner,** founder and CEO, Orange

This book will remind us all about how much children matter to God and should matter to us. Jimmy and Greg are a great tag team for lifting children out of spiritual and physical poverty.

—**Dr. David Anderson,** CEO, BridgeLeader Network; founder and senior pastor, Bridgeway Community Church

This brilliant message can change everything about the strategic place of children in the church and in the kingdom of God, where the little are big, and small matters.

—**Dr. Wess Stafford,** president emeritus, Compassion International

When Jim and Greg have something to say on this and other issues, I listen and act. I encourage you to do the same. Our world and the kingdom will be the better for it.

—**Brian Tome,** Crossroads Church

God is calling us to unleash biblically anchored, Christ-centered, world-changers. Grab this book and get the tools that will equip you to raise up world-changing children.

—**Craig Groeschel,** senior pastor, Life Church

Small Matters

Other Books in the Exponential Series

(More titles forthcoming)

Small Matters

How Churches and Parents Can Raise Up World-Changing Children

Greg Nettle and Santiago "Jimmy" Mellado

ZONDERVAN

Small Matters

Copyright © 2016 by Greg Nettle and Compassion International, Inc.

Requests for information should be addressed to:
Zondervan, 3900 *Sparks Dr. SE, Grand Rapids, Michigan 49546*

Library of Congress Cataloging-in-Publication Data

Names: Nettle, Greg, 1962- author.
Title: Small matters : how churches and parents can raise up world-changing
    children / Greg Nettle and Santiago Mellado.
Description: Grand Rapids : Zondervan, 2016. | Series: Exponential series | Includes
    bibliographical references.
Identifiers: LCCN 2015042926 | ISBN 9780310521037 (softcover)
Subjects: LCSH: Christian education of children. | Parenting—Religious aspects—
    Christianity. | Child rearing—Religious aspects—Christianity.
Classification: LCC BV1475.3 .N48 2016 | DDC 248.8/45—dc23 LC record available
    at http://lccn.loc.gov/2015042926

Unless otherwise noted, Scripture quotations are taken from the *Holy Bible*, New
Living Translation. © 1996, 2004, 2007, 2013 by Tyndale House Foundation. Used by
permission of Tyndale House Publishers, Inc., Carol Stream, Illinois 60188. All rights
reserved.

Scripture quotations marked NIV are taken from The Holy Bible, New International
Version®, NIV®. Copyright © 1973, 1978, 1984, 2011 by Biblica, Inc.® Used by
permission of Zondervan. All rights reserved worldwide. www.Zondervan.com. The
"NIV" and "New International Version" are trademarks registered in the United
States Patent and Trademark Office by Biblica, Inc.®

Scripture quotations marked MSG are taken from *The Message*. Copyright © by
Eugene H. Peterson 1993, 1994, 1995, 1996, 2000, 2001, 2002. Used by permission
of Tyndale House Publishers, Inc.

Any Internet addresses (websites, blogs, etc.) and telephone numbers in this book
are offered as a resource. They are not intended in any way to be or imply an
endorsement by Zondervan, nor does Zondervan vouch for the content of these
sites and numbers for the life of this book.

Cover design: DualIdentity
Cover photos: iStockPhoto, Lightstock, Compassion International
Interior design: Kait Lamphere

Printed in the United States of America

16 17 18 19 20 21 22 23 24 25 26 /DHV/ 15 14 13 12 11 10 9 8 7 6 5 4 3 2 1

Greg:
To Sunshine (Tabitha) and Moonshadow (Elijah)—
the small matters who matter most in my life

Jimmy:
To my adventuresome father and compassionate mother, who
travelled the world extending the love of Jesus to those in need

Contents

Foreword

Someone once asked novelist George MacDonald why he enjoyed writing stories about princesses. "Because every little girl is a princess," he said.

The person asking him the question was confused and wondered what he meant. To clarify, MacDonald posed his own question: "What is a princess?"

"The daughter of a king," the man answered.

"Very well, then," replied MacDonald. "Every little girl *is* a princess." Why? Because McDonald believed that every one of us is a child of a King.

That's why Greg and Jimmy have written this book. They believe that little lives count, that children matter enormously, that they are sacred and should be prized. Though this might seem obvious to some, this truth has not been self-evident to the human race for most of our history. Roman writer Seneca wrote that in ancient Rome, children who were malformed or unhealthy typically were drowned. The Romans killed children who were unwanted or of the wrong gender. Abandoned children were left on a pile of dirt or dung, and though most of them died, occasionally they were rescued, only to live out their days as slaves. This was such a common experience for children at that time that hundreds of names in the ancient world were variations of the Greek word *kopros*, which means "dung."

Yet even as children were being abandoned at the garbage

dump, a quiet revolution had begun. A new movement of people called "the Christians" followed a man who did not despise children or use them as slaves. He took children into his arms and blessed them. He taught his followers that unless a person becomes like a little child, they cannot live in his kingdom, the kingdom of heaven. In the ancient world, where children were frequently ignored and abandoned, no one else praised or valued little children the way this man did.

These early Christians followed a man they believed to be God in the flesh, and yet they believed that God had come to earth and made himself nothing—nothing but an ordinary baby. They were radically transformed by the truth that if God himself could become a humble, dependent infant, then every human life—even the lives of infants and children—was of enormous value. These first followers of Jesus began the practice of giving every child a "godparent," people who promised to raise the children and not abandon them if their parents died. They created orphanages, homes where little children without parents could live instead of fending for themselves. Followers of Jesus know that small *matters*. That children *matter* to God.

The early church forbade the practice of abandoning children by exposure as well as the practices of abortion and infanticide. Their motive, unlike Rome, was not to provide the state with more workers. In the words of one ancient writer, they saved children because "all babies are glorious before God." The early church changed the culture around them, beginning a new and unprecedented era for children. A book that covers this subject is simply titled *When Children Became People: The Birth of Childhood in Early Christianity*.

And yet . . .

Today, suffering falls most heavily on little children. In this book, Greg and Jimmy describe our world, a world in which thousands of children die from preventable diseases each day. We live in a world where illiteracy cripples a child's future, where isolation cripples a child's spirit, where disease cripples a child's body, and where abandonment cripples a child's heart.

But these children are not alone. God has a special place in his heart for them, and God has created a special way of caring for them. *You* and *me*. If you care about the God who came as a child, then you must also care for the children he loves. As they share stories and examples of how to love children, Jimmy and Greg aren't simply alerting us to the dangers that children face. Yes, this book speaks about heartbreak and struggle, but it is also a book about hope. More has been done in recent years to alleviate the poverty that hurts children than the world thought possible a generation ago. And what if that work might be carried even further? What if we were able to see it through to completion? What if God might be calling you to be part of this cause?

And the goal is not simply the elimination of physical poverty. There is a poverty of spirit that robs children of hope and goodness and joy, and the gospel speaks powerfully to this need. This is why the church was born.

This is a book about small matters, which are really large matters that are far greater than our greatest dreams. God has used the small things of this world to do his work, and he continues to do this today. In Jesus' kingdom, the first are last and the least are the greatest, the servants are the heroes and the small are the biggest winners of all.

—*John Ortberg, author and pastor*

CHAPTER 1

Children at Risk

Don't give up! I believe in you all! A person's a
person no matter how small! And you very small
persons will not have to die if you make yourselves
heard! So come on, now, and TRY!

—Dr. Seuss, *Horton Hears a Who*

[Jesus] said to them, "The child is not dead but
asleep."

—Mark 5:39 NIV

Every child is at risk.

There are dangers and diseases that stem from poverty, and
there are dangers and diseases that stem from prosperity.

Throughout our travels to some of the darkest recesses of
poverty on the planet, we've witnessed firsthand the dangers and
diseases that stem from poverty. And as a result of raising children
in the United States, we've also witnessed firsthand the dangers
and diseases that stem from prosperity.

We've seen children eat dirt to fill their rumbling stomachs,
and we've seen children struggling with obesity from too many
trips to the nearest fast-food chain restaurant. We've paddled a
canoe through sewage-polluted waters to reach the home of a child
in Ecuador, and we've driven our SUVs to cavernous "mansions" to
visit children lost in a sea of suburban materialism in the US, living
in homes filled with lots of stuff, but very little love. We've walked

into rooms where two adults and five children share a single bed, crowded in a small space, and we've been in rooms where a single bed holds a child searching for purpose.

We've surveyed the emotional damage that results from broken families, and have found that it doesn't matter whether you live in poverty or prosperity. The results are the same. We've seen firsthand the pain of alcohol abuse by fathers and mothers. We've watched as families are shattered when marriages end in divorce. We've witnessed families ravaged by greed. We've seen the despair that grows in the hearts of children when they face seemingly hopeless situations. It doesn't matter whether your family is poor or prosperous—every child is at risk.

Fourteen-year-old Tabitha is at risk growing up in the prosperity of the United States. Six-year-old Kizel is at risk growing up in the poverty of Bolivia. On any given night, Tabitha goes to bed worrying about bullying, popularity, test scores, and what she is going to wear tomorrow. Every day, she is exposed to the dangers and diseases of prosperity. On any given night, Kizel goes to bed worrying about the boys across the street, how she will make it in this world, who she can trust, and what she will wear tomorrow. Every day, she is exposed to the dangers and diseases of poverty. If you read closely, you'll notice that both girls suffer similar risks.

We see poverty and prosperity as similar problems. Though the circumstances of a child in poverty are different from those of a child in prosperity, they are both equally at risk. One child has too little. One child has too much. One child needs more. One child *thinks* she deserves more. One child is in danger of forgetting about God because she doesn't have enough. One child is in danger of forgetting about God because she has more than enough.

Most everyone will say, "We need to care for kids." It's a platitude that bounces off the ears, we hear it so often. Politicians appeal to children to attract people to their cause. They champion their position by saying, "It's for the children." "Children are our future." "No child left behind." "Our children are counting on us." Can you imagine any politician getting elected if they stopped the endless promises? "No more for the children; they have enough." It's never going to happen.

We all say that we care about children. But caring about children requires more than a feel-good slogan. On the continuum of poverty to prosperity, children need critical interventions appropriate to the conditions they face. Those who raise children in poverty face many challenges—physical needs, emotional needs, social needs. Raising a child in poverty entails many risks, and we don't want to minimize the hardship of living in extreme poverty. We want to call readers of this book, many of whom likely come from more prosperous backgrounds, to get involved in fighting the risks of poverty.

But we also want to draw your attention to the risks of prosperity. They pose a particular challenge as well. And how we meet that challenge shapes the kind of children who leave our homes and enter the world as adults.

At first, it might be difficult to see the risks of prosperity. Money and wealth provide so many advantages to a child that we think the risks are minimal at best. Yet this thinking reveals our cultural blindness. Every day, children living in prosperity risk losing God's perspective on the world. We go through the motions, keep busy, and never question our routines of prosperity.

Preschools and high schools. Athletics. Music. Scouting. Mobile devices. Full refrigerators. Even fuller closets. First cars. Second cars. A three-car garage. Youth groups. Universities. Community colleges. Financial aid. Internships. Entertainment. Free time. Hiking trails. Jet skis. Snow skis. Emergency rooms. (These last two go together!)

First World Problems?

In recent years, people have begun using social media to complain about the "problems" they face in wealthier nations like the United States. Here are a few examples:

- **Privilege:** "I didn't get the car I wanted for my sixteenth birthday."
- **Selfishness:** "No, he can't play with one of my many toy trucks!"
- **Abundance:** *(Child staring into a refrigerator full of food.)* "Mom, there's nothing to eat."
- **Ingratitude:** "I don't want to go to church today."
- **Expectations:** "I *need* those new shoes for the school dance."
- **Entitlement:** "The internet is running too slow. I'm having a hard time playing games on my iPad."

We agree that people living in prosperity often lose perspective and take much of their comfort and wealth for granted. Yet the answer is not to mock; instead, the answer is to deepen everyone's awareness of the very real problems of prosperity. They are different from the problems faced by the poor, but they are real dangers that kids need help to avoid. We've written this book to help you see that every child is at risk.

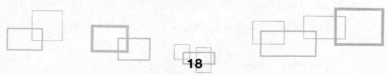

Our children have many hobbies, interests, and privileges—all the wonderful fruits of prosperity.

Most of this blessing and privilege is assumed. We take it for granted that we have options, that it's all there for the choosing. If we pay any attention to these things at all, it's to offer critique when they disappoint and to complain when things don't work as we've come to expect them to. The overwhelming majority of us live in—and recline on—these fantastic "cushions of provision."

We must be grateful. But we must not be naive.

Prosperity can leak toxins into the lives of our kids. We see it pollute attitudes with a sense of entitlement. We see children who have everything a child could want still discontented. We see kids who are surrounded by multiple video-game consoles dealing with boredom. And most important is how prosperity numbs our need for God, leading to a lack of dependence on God.

When we encounter children living in poverty, we look for solutions to their poverty. We look for ways to move them away from the problems they face. If they lack food, we seek to provide nutritious meals or to develop means within the community to enable greater self-sufficiency. If they lack education, we seek to provide schooling to enable opportunity for economic advancement. If they lack medical care, we arrange for doctors and nurses and set a goal of constructing a medical center. If they have never heard about Jesus, we do our best to help plant a new church. We see the risks and seek to provide solutions.

Just as we seek to move kids away from the damages of abject poverty, we need to engineer experiences for kids living in prosperity that can help to move them away from their self-centeredness. We need to expose them to opportunities that challenge them to serve rather than to be served, to give rather than receive, to share their abundance rather than hoard. We need to provide opportunities for them to tell others about Jesus rather than just sit in church listening to someone tell them about Jesus. We need to give them opportunities to discover their own needs and to learn to seek God to provide for them.

Here is an illustration of what we mean.

Greg was traveling in San Francisco when he received this text from his wife: "Children released from school. Bomb threat. Tabitha home safely." The text was brief and unexpected, but it ended with the words Greg needed to hear more than anything. His daughter was safe. Two minutes before the final period of the school day ended, the principal had announced that all students must evacuate the high school. "Do not return to your lockers. Do not look for friends. Proceed immediately to the parking lot." Someone had called to say that a bomb was in the school. Not knowing whether that was true, the principal had wisely removed the children from the potential danger. As you can imagine, this was a traumatic experience for Greg's daughter, Tabitha, and for her parents!

The bomb threat was unexpected. The Nettles live in a quiet bedroom community in northern Ohio. And even though no bomb was discovered, when a threat appeared, the school took action. When children's lives are at stake, you don't delay; you act. In this case, a school full of children was at risk and immediate action was needed.

The dangers children face today are real. They have life-or-death consequences. If we evacuate a school at the threat of a bomb, should we not take these other risks—the risks of growing up blind to the dangers of prosperity—with equal, if not greater, seriousness?

Elisabeth's Story (Jimmy)

Early on, Leanne and I decided our kids didn't need to hear another sermon on gratefulness. Growing up in the United States, they were surrounded by the comforts of our prosperous lifestyle. What they needed was a personal connection to kids who didn't have those comforts, to children with far less. They needed to broaden their social network to include relationships in which they could expand their global view of reality and learn to care and to give. Long before I came to work for Compassion International (a ministry dedicated to holistic child development through sponsorship), we decided to involve our kids in the Compassion program. We wanted to link our kids to what God was doing in the lives of other children around the world.

One evening when our kids were in middle school and high school, we sat down as a family to talk about sponsoring a child. Leanne and I explained what it was like to sponsor a child, and we made it clear that if we did this, it would be a family activity. Everyone would be involved. There would be no disinterested spectators. We would fund it, but our kids were to reach out and become friends with their sponsored child.

Leanne and I organized it all. We suggested that each of our children select a child with their same name to help them feel a more personal connection with each child our family was sponsoring. Since that family meeting, we've sponsored nine children.

We started by selecting the country of Guatemala and logging on to the Compassion website. The kids went to work. Our youngest, David, chose a young boy named David Nehemiahs. Elisabeth discovered Elisabeth Carolina. And Ester connected with Nayeli Estrellita (Estrellita means "little star"). In the years that followed, each of these relationships became long-distance friendships. Each child benefited the other as they grew in their understanding. For the Mellados, it was a way to see the world through the eyes of children living in poverty. This shift in perspective became one strategic way to help move our children from an attitude of entitlement to one of compassion and understanding. We wanted them to move from taking to giving, from spectating to investing. We knew that the subtle toxic leaks of prosperity can be diluted only in the waters of sharing.

Our daughter Elisabeth, or Bizzy, as we call her, experienced this shift in perspective in dramatic fashion. Soon after Bizzy began her sponsorship, she received terrible news about her namesake's father in Guatemala. He had fallen from a tree, broken his back, and was incapacitated. We had an opportunity to visit Guatemala and see the family, and it broke our hearts to see the father restricted to life in bed, his hands frozen and atrophied. We could not forget the deadness in his eyes. Work was impossible. For a family living in extreme poverty, this was devastating.

But things got even worse.

Elisabeth's mother died unexpectedly. This was crushing for the family, and Elisabeth instantly became a twelve-year-old caregiver for her three younger siblings. Her childhood had been taken away from her as she was thrust into the overwhelming responsibilities of adulthood.

Months later, we were encouraged to hear that Elisabeth's father was slowly healing. Eventually, he was able to work, and he found a job. Unfortunately, it was across the border in Mexico, so he was gone for weeks at a time. This transformed Elisabeth into the sole caregiver to her younger siblings.

The government intervened and moved Elisabeth and her siblings out of their community and into institutions in Guatemala City, breaking up the little family. Although Elisabeth's father was doing all he could do to provide for them, Elisabeth and her siblings needed help.

Our Bizzy also needed help. Without her connection to Elisabeth and her family in Guatemala that exposed her to the suffering of the world, Bizzy was in danger of growing up with a sense of entitlement, of mistaking God's blessings for rights and privileges.

By bridging the gap between their two lives—Elisabeth in Guatemala, Bizzy in the US—we were able to shine a small light of understanding to help each girl realize her need for God and find hope through Jesus. I'm going to share more about this story later in the book.

Danger by the Numbers

All children are exposed to the violence of life. Some witness it firsthand. Others experience it through the media. An average American child will see 200,000 violent acts and 16,000 murders on TV by age eighteen.[1] Worldwide, hundreds of thousands of children have been recruited into government armed forces, paramilitaries, civil militia, and a variety of other armed groups.[2] More than 5.5 million children in Syria have faced the ravages of ongoing wars and violent civil unrest.[3] Many children live in communities where terrorism is a nearly constant threat.

Sometimes violence keeps children from the benefits afforded them by a good education. This is true even in the United States. In the US, 7.1 percent of students did not go to school on one or more days in the preceding thirty days because they felt unsafe at school or on their way to or from school, according to a Centers for Disease Control survey. In addition, 20.1 percent of students reported being bullied on school property in the twelve months preceding the survey. It should be noted that the prevalence was higher among females (8.7 percent) than males (5.4 percent).[4] In developing countries, 13 percent of children between the ages of seven and eighteen have never even attended school.[5]

Children today are increasingly vulnerable to sexual violence. Many are victims of sexual abuse. More than 100,000 children living in the US are sold into sex trafficking every year.[6] In Europe, 18 million children under the age of eighteen suffer from sexual abuse. In Australia, one in three girls and one in six boys will be sexually abused in some way before the age of eighteen.[7] This is a global plague. Every year 2 million children around the world are exploited in commercial sex trafficking.[8]

The harsh realities of childhood in developing countries are sobering. A staggering 400 million children around the world are living in extreme poverty (defined as living on less than $1.25 per day).[9] One in three children in the developing world—more than 500 million children—have no access to sanitation facilities. And some 400 million children, one in five, have no access to safe water, and unsafe water and lack of sanitation cause about 4,000 child deaths per day,[10] deaths that might still be preventable if not for the fact that 270 million children have no access to health care.[11] The solution to these problems is not simple. The truth is that if you construct a hospital, you also have to make sure the hospital has water. And if the hospital has water, you then have to ensure safe sanitation and sewage treatment. These challenges are difficult, even daunting, but they are not impossible.

Every day, 21,000 children die as a result of poverty or poverty-related preventable diseases. Every 3.6 seconds, a person dies of starvation, and most often it is a child under the age of five.[12] And while the toll of excess in prosperous communities and countries may be less tragic and is more difficult to quantify, there is a cost. In 2013, 42 million infants and children in the world were overweight or obese, and an estimated 70 million will be by 2025, leading to various chronic and even fatal health problems, including diabetes and heart disease.[13] As our mentor Dr. Wess Stafford repeatedly states, "Satan's strategy is to go after the weakest and most vulnerable people on the planet . . . our children."

And Satan's strategy appears to be working. What can we do?

Finding Hope

A fascinating story about Jesus is recounted in Luke, chapter 8. Jesus had a crowd around him when a man named Jairus approached him. Jairus fell at Jesus' feet and begged him to come to his home because his twelve-year-old daughter—his only child—was dying. So Jesus starts pushing his way through the throng of people in an attempt to make it to the man's home.

People were clamoring for Jesus' attention. They wanted *their* needs met. They were hungry for healing. They were reaching out to touch him. At one point Jesus stops, and a woman who had been ill for years is healed. At that point, a servant from Jairus's household came to him and exclaimed, "Your daughter died. There's no need to bother Jesus now."

All hope seemed to be gone. What could be worse than the death of your only child? But Jesus responds, "Don't be upset." (Seriously?) "Just trust me and everything will be all right." So Jesus and Jairus continue on their journey.

When they arrive at Jairus's home, family and friends are outside weeping. Jesus walks up to them and says, "Don't cry. She didn't die. She's just sleeping." And everyone laughs at him.

Jesus walks into the house. He takes the little girl by the hand and says, "My dear child, get up." And in that instant, she is up and breathing again!

Jesus loves children. He is the One who calls children from death to life. Jesus is the One who rouses children from hopeless sleep to joyful awakening. Jesus is the One who invites you and me to join him in reaching out to children the world has given up on, to take them by the hand, to rejoice for this one others considered lost who has found the way home.

It's easy to overlook children. They are small. Their world seems so small. They may not appear to have much to offer us in return. But Jesus is the One who teaches us that small matters. Children matter to God, and while every child is at risk . . . there is hope. Our colleague Dr. Scott Todd has written extensively about positive trends in the developing world in his wonderful book *Hope Rising*:[14]

- In only eight years, from 2000 to 2008, the number of kids dying from measles has declined by 78 percent (from 733,000 deaths per year to 164,000) because we are completing the work of immunizing every child.[15]

- Twenty-two countries have cut their malaria rates in half in only six years. They did it by using insecticide-treated bed nets, accessing better medicines, and spraying to kill mosquitoes. Globally, malaria infections have decreased by 19 million per year, and malaria deaths have dropped by 140,000 per year between 2005 and 2009.[16]

- We used to say that 40,000 children die each day from preventable causes. In the 1990s, that number dropped to 33,000 per day. By 2008, it dropped to 24,000. It is now down to 21,000. The number of children dying before their fifth birthday has been cut in half, and it was done in one generation, using a wide range of practical strategies, from creating access to clean water to training skilled birth attendants.[17]

- A third of the children who were uneducated because of poverty can now go to school. Literacy rates are climbing. Those gains were made in less than ten years.[18]

- Today there are about 1.4 billion people living in extreme poverty. And that's good news. In 1981, 52 percent of the world's population lived in extreme poverty. Today that number is 21 percent, reducing the number by more than half! And it was accomplished in one generation.[19]

But these stats tell only part of the story. What we are seeing in the developed world is that *global awareness* is on the rise. Today, schools are including global studies in their required curriculum for students. The rise of the internet and the availability of global news have made us all more aware of the needs of the world's population and the risks facing children. Recent studies show that Millennials, those born between 1980 and 2000, tend to be more interested in making a positive change in society than they are in becoming part of the corporate structure and simply making money.[20] In his book *Meet the Millennials*, Leigh Buchanan writes, "One of the characteristics of Millennials, besides the fact that they are masters of digital communication, is that they are primed to do well by doing good. Almost 70 percent say that giving back and being civically engaged are their highest priorities."[21]

Consider the story of twenty-nine-year-old Leigh Madeira. Her dream is to help find funding for young companies devoted to improving the lives of the world's poor. That isn't quite what her family had in mind when they sent her off to college. When she told her ninety-year-old grandfather about her plans, "He gave me this look," she said, laughing.

For Madeira and others in her generation, the goal of a high-priced business degree isn't a job in traditional Wall Street finance anymore. Many are embracing "socially responsible" investing, which steers money to businesses and organizations that pledge to have a positive effect on society and the planet.[22]

This global vision and interest in reaching around the globe to help those in need cannot be left to Wall Street. It needs to be matched with God's vision for the world, his Great Commission for his church. Today, we are seeing an increased energy and enthusiasm for church planting. This is true not only in North America but also in both developed and developing countries around the world. Since new church planting remains the single most effective way to reach people with the good news of Jesus Christ, this is a wonderful trend to celebrate. Even better, many new church plants are launching with a strategy to care for children. The global church-planting organization that Greg leads, Stadia, now requires every one of its new church plants to have a strategic plan for how they will care for children, locally and around the world. It's distinctive of Stadia's ministry and its partnership with Compassion International. In fact, having a plan to care for children is one of the reasons we are writing this book. We've become aware of a significant reality: 85 percent of those who choose to follow Jesus do so between the ages of four and fourteen. We believe this strategy—to plant churches that reach children in this age group—has the potential to dramatically and radically change the results of new church plantings.[23]

Hope for the Church and Children

Scott and Vanessa Pugh planted Velocity Church in South Euclid, Ohio, six years ago. "The schools call me for everything," Scott says. "We chaperone the dances. I speak every year for the National Honor Society induction. We run the XLR8 program that teaches kids how to be healthy on social media." Several of the Cleveland Browns run a free football camp for Scott for second to sixth graders every year. Recently, Notre Dame College in South Euclid contacted Scott to ask if Velocity would plant a church on their campus to care for their students.

In addition to the ministry they have in planting Velocity and future churches, Scott and Vanessa also sponsor two children through Compassion International. This means that each of their sponsored children is known, loved, and protected by a church in their own neighborhood. These sponsorships provide holistic care to make sure each child receives an education and tutoring, regular health checkups, and health training. These local churches also provide a safe place for children to play and interact with other children and to hear about the love of Jesus in personal, age-appropriate ways. One of their sponsored children is in Ecuador and one is in Africa. And Scott and Vanessa's concern for these children spills over into their ministry in their church. They have had five Compassion Sundays in their church, Sundays that focus attention on the needs of some of the world's neediest children and invite people to embrace a Compassion sponsorship—one family supporting one child.

The leaders at Velocity are committed to raising up the value of children throughout their entire church. Children are an integral part of Velocity's ministry teams, serving on the worship team, greeting team, food-prep team, communion prep, and offering collection. In addition to his weekend preaching responsibilities, Scott teaches in the weekly children's ministry, Kids' City, at least ten times a year.

Another great example of a young church highlighting the value and importance of children is Bart and Jodi Stone's church plant, Momentum Church, in the greater Atlanta area. The Stones decided right from the start to develop a dynamic children's ministry. Their biological son, Keaton, was five when Momentum began, and that year the Stones journeyed to China to adopt their daughter Addison. Seven years later, they returned to China to bring home their second daughter, Lexi. Their example in caring for children through adoption has inspired numerous others in their church to adopt as well.

The Stones' heart for children and their global vision for those in need and for families who have not heard the gospel prompted Momentum Church to partner with both Stadia and Compassion to plant a church in Manta, Ecuador. The people of Momentum now sponsor more than two hundred children through Compassion International, many of whom now attend the new Ecuadorian church Momentum helped to start. Bart said that meeting his two sponsored children in Ecuador was one of the greatest things he has ever been able to do. Their church doesn't believe children are the church of tomorrow; they believe children are the church of today.

Some leaders may wonder how a focus on children is possible when their church doesn't have any young families. Our response: Get creative. Don't just focus on who is attending church now. Reach out. Begin caring for kids in your community. Some churches have had success in tapping into the passion and energy of young adults. Ben and Shaina Thompson launched City Campus Church on the edge of the Ohio State University campus. Even though the majority of their new church is college students, the church is deeply committed to caring for children. They partnered with the middle school in which they meet for services to care for the students of that school. Now other schools throughout Columbus are asking City Church to launch a new church in their schools! City Campus started serving the schools simply by providing punch and cookies for the eighth-grade graduation. Next came helping with school maintenance. Soon they were asked to run the after-school program to tutor students. Every year City Campus fills backpacks with supplies for under-resourced students. In their first year, instead of spending money on marketing, they packed twenty thousand meals in two hours for Columbus City Schools for students who needed meals on weekends.

And all of this local outreach to children has a corresponding global focus. In just the first two years of City Campus's existence, they have helped plant two new churches in Latin America—both of which partner with Stadia and Compassion International. All of this is happening in a church that doesn't have many young children!

We share these stories to give you a taste of the amazing changes we are seeing in churches around the world. Over the past five years, ninety new churches have been planted in partnerships between Stadia, one of the largest global church-planting ministries, and Compassion International. This partnership has focused on planting new churches and starting new Compassion ministries throughout Latin America. Each of these ninety new churches cares for at least two hundred sponsored children, and for each child sponsored, that new church has credible access to at least thirty additional people living in their community. Do the math and you'll see that 90 churches × 200 children × 30 people = 540,000 people. This work over the past five years has touched the lives of more than fifty thousand people with the good news of Jesus Christ, and it all began with the conviction that children matter to God—*small matters!* This number doesn't begin to take into account the thousands of lives that are being transformed in the United States as a result of planting new churches and sponsoring children.

While Satan's strategy is to attack the weakest and most

vulnerable among us—our children—we can use Satan's strategy against him by serving the needs of the smallest and weakest. And we can witness the spread of the gospel to new communities—all through ministry to children.

Audacious Vision

Brian Tome is the dynamic, outspoken leader of Crossroads Community Church in Cincinnati. This large multicampus church ministers in many amazing ways. Recently, Brian accepted an invitation to travel to Nicaragua with friends from Compassion International and with TV producers Mark Burnett and Roma Downey of *The Bible* TV series. The trip gave Brian an opportunity to see the plight of children living in poverty and the amazing power that is unleashed when the local church releases children from those chains through a program of holistic child development.

For four days, Brian visited churches and child development centers and talked to children. He crammed into tiny homes and met moms, dads, grandparents, and caregivers. Brian let God shape his perspective. By the time his plane was lifting off from Managua, he had already charted a new flight path for his congregation. He would host Crossroads' first-ever Compassion Sunday.

Compassion would have been thrilled for Brian to loft a challenge to his church to sponsor a thousand children through Compassion. Two thousand would have been beyond any expectations. But Brian set an audacious goal: four thousand children sponsored in a single weekend. When that weekend came, Brian was articulate, passionate, and pointed in his challenge to the church. "We have the resources," he told the Crossroads congregation. "It's just that our heart isn't about what God's is about." The church responded. Hearts came alive to bring hope to children in poverty.

It turns out Brian's big audacious goal of faith was actually a bit smaller than God's. A total of 5,972 children received sponsors that weekend!

Tabitha and Kizel

Sponsoring a child isn't just for adults—even the smallest can make a difference. Two years ago, when Greg's daughter, Tabitha, was just fourteen, she started sponsoring six-year-old Kizel, who was part of a new church plant in Bolivia. Tabitha now prays for Kizel. She sends letters and gifts to Kizel. She sends money she earns from babysitting to pay for Kizel's sponsorship. This new relationship with Kizel has been a way for Tabitha to show her friend the love of Jesus. And Kizel, living in poverty in Bolivia, prays for Tabitha. She sends letters to Tabitha. She is going to school and is part of a new local church. Her life has been forever changed by her relationship with her sister in Christ, Tabitha, and with Jesus. As a result, both girls are less at risk.

This is a movement to help children that we are seeing all around the globe. Pastors, leaders, and Jesus followers in their communities are more aware of global needs and are hungry to do something by ministering to the weakest, smallest, and most vulnerable people in our world. Each church must start small, because "small" matters to the heart of God.

Our Prayer

Throughout this book we will talk about caring for children in our homes, in the communities where we live, and around the world through new opportunities—sponsorship of children and the planting of new churches that care for kids.

Small Matters

Our prayer is that as you read, God will open your eyes to show you how much small matters. We hope that the needs of children will become a pebble in your shoe. A kernel of corn stuck in your teeth. Sand in your bed. A blister on your big toe. A splinter in your finger. We hope that the thought of caring for kids excites you and even frustrates you and that it ultimately moves you—to do something about it.

CHAPTER 2

Wrecked
(Greg's Story)

May God break my heart so completely that the whole world falls in.

—Mother Teresa

Me: "God, why don't you do something?"
God: "I did. I created you."

—Matthew West

I sat in Wess Stafford's office with my head in my hands. *How could I have missed this?*

How could I have missed the fact that children are close to the heart of God? After leading a thriving megachurch in northern Ohio for fifteen years. After earning seminary and graduate school degrees. After having a daughter of my own . . .

Wess was serving as president of Compassion International, an extraordinary child development ministry that brings hope to children around the world in Jesus' name. Wess's compassion flowed out to me. He said, "I am so glad that God has wrecked your heart for his kids."

As lead pastor of RiverTree Christian Church, I had insisted that we have the best children's programs in our area. Even if the classes were full, we never turned away a child at one of our weekend services. And we worked hard to make sure the kids had fun! Why? Because if children loved coming to RiverTree, then we knew their parents would want to return. If we could win the children, we could win the parents and build a great church. For me, children were a means to an end.

On numerous occasions, an advocate for Compassion International had asked me to incorporate a child-sponsorship event into our weekend services. I repeatedly told him "absolutely not." I was concerned that if I encouraged people to sponsor children, then those same people would divert their funding away from the ministries of our church. In my role as senior pastor, one of my top priorities was to keep the financial engine of RiverTree fueled. It wasn't that I didn't value the ministry of Compassion. I just knew that I was responsible for *our* church, for *our* ministries, and I didn't see why it was necessary to publicly partner with another ministry. We had our own goals and priorities to support.

So how did I end up sitting on Wess Stafford's couch with my heart absolutely wrecked over children? It all started with a book, much like the one you are reading now. Our executive pastor had given me a copy of Wess's book *Too Small to Ignore*[1] and said, "I think you should read this."

A Nudge toward Children

I finished reading the book on Thanksgiving evening that year. I wept. Not tears rolling gently down my cheeks; rather, the floodgates were opened. God's work in my heart had begun. One reason for my tears was simple theology. In his book, Wess pointed me to the countless references in the Bible where God speaks of our responsibility to care for children. The other reason for my tears was Wess's story. He described candidly the risks he faced as a missionary's child in Africa. His story tore me up. But what really messed with me was a growing awareness of all the children throughout the United States and around the world with real needs, needs I was ignoring in my efforts to lead our church. How could I care so little when God cares so much about these children?

I called Gary, our executive pastor, and told him that I thought God wanted me to meet with Wess Stafford—in Colorado. Gary said he would do his best to set it up. "One question though," he said. "When they want to know why you want to meet with Wess, what should I tell them?"

"I have no idea," I responded. "Just tell them I believe God wants me to meet him."

I arrived at Compassion's offices in Colorado Springs two weeks later. Wess's executive assistant, Angie, asked, "So why are you meeting with Wess?"

"I have no idea," I answered. "I just believe that God wants me to be here to spend some time with him."

She smiled.

After my initial breakdown on Wess's couch, we talked for two hours. Wess talked about growing up in Africa and how his African friends—children—died simply because they had been born into poverty. You probably think I'm a blubbering idiot, but the truth is that I had never been a crier—especially not over the plight of children. Yet after hearing more of Wess's story, my heart was moved with compassion and a desire to do something. I began to understand that there were things I could do. I could make a difference in the lives of children.

At the end of our time together, Wess suggested that we pray. After we spent time talking with God, I said to Wess, "I know how subjective this is, but during our prayer time, I sensed God telling me that I was supposed to ask you to mentor me."

Wess replied, "During our prayer time, I sensed God telling me that I was supposed to pour my life into this young man."

And so our journey began.

God has continued to wreck my heart in new ways for children at risk, and I have done my best to respond. I began by leading our church to sponsor children. During our first Compassion Sunday, the church sponsored several hundred children. Today that number has grown to more than 2,800! And my worries about redirecting finances away from our church were foolish. In all this time, RiverTree has never missed paying a bill and, in fact, has grown extravagantly in generosity. Our focus on children at risk has raised the value of children not only globally but also in our local community. At one time, we had to beg church members to work in our children's programs. Now we have a thriving children's ministry filled with amazing servants who teach and love our children. I always smile when I see men walking our church hallways wearing T-shirts that say, *Real men serve in TreeHouse Kidz.*

My wife, Julie, and I sponsored our first Compassion child, Inte, more than ten years ago. We have visited Inte in her home country of Ecuador numerous times, but I'll never forget my first visit with Inte. We were on a bus with several other sponsors and their sponsored children. I pulled a bag of individually wrapped Now and Later candies from my backpack, handed them to Inte, and helped her open the bag. Inte quickly stood up and gave candy to every child and adult on the bus. When she returned, she showed me the empty bag. She had not saved a single piece for herself! This was the first of many lessons I learned from the children. The generosity of God was visible in Inte's words and actions, and I learned that you cannot outgive the poor. Those who are poor in material possessions recognize God's provision and must give what they can. Those who are rich in material possessions recognize their danger of spiritual poverty and must give as much as they can.

Greg and Wess in Ecuador

I traveled with Wess into countries where Compassion had ministries. I learned from him not only about God's heart for those who are living in poverty but also about my responsibility to care for the children that God had placed in my own immediate care. Wess has often said, "We never stand so tall as when we stoop to bless a child." I have learned that this is true, whether we are serving the poor in Africa or our own children in our own homes.

Under Our Own Roof

In the United States, nearly 400,000 children are in our foster-care system. These are children who desperately need to have the love of Jesus shared with them in a tangible way. As I was learning about the needs of children and God was opening my eyes to his heart for them, a natural next step for my wife, Julie, and me was to consider becoming foster parents. We started by asking the hard question: "If we don't care for these children, who will?

Because we lead extremely busy lives, I sometimes jokingly tell people that we decided to do this because we didn't have anything else to do. It is a big commitment! To become a foster parent in the state of Ohio, you must complete forty hours of training *every* year. It is not an easy process, but it is worth the effort. Instead of caring for children full-time, we offer respite care, keeping a foster child in our home for two to three nights, which allows the foster parents to have a short break. This ministry to these children in our home has become one of the richest experiences of our lives.

We've also seen the power of hosting international students and children for short periods of time. One weekend our church hosted the African Children's Choir, young African children who travel throughout the world performing amazing musical concerts. The children in the choir see the opportunities and possibilities available in the world outside their villages. Their audiences learn about the plight of the poor in Africa.

After the first concert, Julie and I met the two little girls who would be staying in our home for the weekend. We brought the girls home, enjoyed a meal together (they cleaned their plates because they will not waste food), and told them as best we could that we were blessed to have them stay with us.

The next day we encouraged our daughter, Tabitha (who was six at the time), to play with her new friends. At first she didn't know what to do. We brought out plain white paper and crayons and suggested that Tabitha bring down some of her sticker collection—a prize possession! She brought down a couple of sheets of stickers, but we asked her to consider sharing more. Begrudgingly, she returned with her entire collection. Much to Tabitha's horror, the girls began to pick her absolute favorite stickers for their coloring pages!

On our final morning together, our two houseguests presented Tabitha with their works of art. Using the crayons, paper, and stickers, they had made beautiful thank-you cards for Tabitha. They hadn't kept any stickers for themselves; they had used them to make the cards for our daughter.

After the African Children's Choir visited our church, we hosted the Romanian Orphans Choir. Both choirs did far more than entertain our congregation. They planted seeds of hope and a vision for adoption that soon spread throughout our church family. Two of our closest friends felt God calling them to adopt. Brett and Sonja had hosted two young boys from the Romanian Orphans Choir. It was a fairly simple responsibility: bring the boys home, share a meal, provide them with a place to sleep, and return them to the church the following morning. But that night changed their lives forever.

Brett and Sonja had two young boys of their own. Sonja told me that as she was preparing their two guests for bed, she told them, "We have set up your beds in our children's toy room." After saying those words, she felt sickened. Here were two boys who didn't own any toys, much less need an entire room to store them. Seeds had been planted. Something shifted in her heart. She felt a burden that became somewhat oppressive. She called the church to ask if anyone there knew anything about adoption. Just asking that question told her she was on the right path. Brett and Sonja adopted a little girl named Anna from Kazakhstan. On the day they brought her home, Julie and I drove to the Pittsburgh Airport and waited in the arrival area with several other family members and friends. When Sonja walked off the plane carrying Anna, her two young sons (who had stayed at home) ran and embraced their parents and their new little sister. People walking past stopped and cheered the emotional reunion. It is a moment that God indelibly etched on my heart. And it was the beginning of the next step in our own journey of caring for children at risk.

Sonja and her adopted daughter Anna

Julie and I began to pray about adopting. Unfortunately, we weren't on the same page. Julie was leaning toward international adoption. I was leaning toward domestic. I explained to her that I sensed God was calling us to adopt a black baby boy from Detroit. (I don't know why Detroit or why black. But I am committed to listening to what I believe God is telling me.) We instead began the tedious process of filling out the paperwork to adopt internationally. We paid filing fees and went to classes. That's when God began to speak to Julie's heart, so we called our local foster care agency, the Christian Children's Home of Ohio. We explained that we believed God was calling us to adopt. They were very encouraging. We said that we believed God was calling us to adopt a black baby boy from Detroit. At that, they were skeptical. They explained that African American babies were rarely available for adoption. Most of the children are kept within the extended family. But they would record our desires and work toward fulfilling them. Once again we began filling out the paperwork, enduring home studies, and attending classes.

Three months later, our caseworker contacted us with a bit of surprise in her voice. "You're not going to believe this," she said. "A young African American mom in Cleveland is going to give birth in two months and wants to put her baby up for adoption."

"Cleveland is close enough to Detroit for me!" I responded.

The two months passed quickly. The day came for the birth-mom to deliver the little boy who would become our son. Then, in the middle of the afternoon, our caseworker called. The birth-mom had given birth to a healthy baby boy, but she had changed her mind and decided to keep him. We were devastated. But we remembered that we had wanted a child who did not have a home. This baby now had a home. So we fought against our disappointment and sadness, and we trusted God.

Two weeks later I was at a leadership gathering in Dallas when Julie called. "You're not going to believe this. The birth-mom brought her baby home, and after two weeks decided she could not care for him. She put him into the foster care system for adoption. Our caseworker just called and asked if we would still be willing to adopt him!"

"Yes! Of course! Yes!" I replied.

One week later, Julie and I drove to Cleveland to meet our new son and bring him home. We were on pins and needles, fearing that the birth-mom would again change her mind, but she did not. I remember holding Elijah in my arms for the first time and sobbing. God was continuing to wreck my heart. Today Elijah is a thriving seven-year-old and a wondrous part of our family. One of my favorite pictures of him is from just before our daughter's freshman homecoming. Tabitha is in her long dress, and Elijah is wearing sweats and rubber boots. They are dancing together on the driveway, expressions of joy on their faces. He is black. She is white. For me, this is a snapshot of what heaven will be like.

Partnering to Love Children

Today, if you were to drive by our church's (RiverTree) largest campus in Jackson Township, Ohio, you would see fourteen thirty-foot flagpoles on the front lawn flying a variety of international flags. Some people might think it's a United Nations building. Each flag represents a country from which a family in our church has adopted a child. When a family brings home their new child, we gather with the family and their friends, and the adopting family raises the flag representing their child's home country. Today, more than two hundred RiverTree families have adopted either domestically or internationally.

Through the ministry of adoption, God has deepened my understanding of his Word. Consider these words in Ephesians: "All praise to God, the Father of our Lord Jesus Christ, who has blessed us with every spiritual blessing in the heavenly realms because we are united with Christ. Even before he made the world, God loved us and chose us in Christ to be holy and without fault in his eyes. God decided in advance to adopt us into his own family by bringing us to himself through Jesus Christ. This is what he wanted to do, and it gave him great pleasure" (Eph. 1:3–5).

Now, having an adopted son and seeing the amazing beauty of adoption in our church family, I understand God's love more clearly than I ever did before. Every one of us has been adopted by God. God loves us the way I love my adopted son! How can we do any less for the children of this world who are still in need of a forever family?

My point in sharing these stories is not to suggest that we all serve in the same way. Some people may sense God calling them to adopt a child. Others may feel a call to foster care. Still others may sense a call to serve children through helping as a volunteer at a vacation Bible school, sponsoring a child through Compassion, or tutoring at a local elementary school. My point is to remind you that God's heart beats for children. They are at the center of his work in this world.

But my story isn't finished yet. Little did I know that when it came to caring for children, God had something more he wanted to do with me. In the summer of 2011, while I was still serving as senior pastor of RiverTree Christian Church, I was asked to become the president of a global church-planting organization called Stadia. Over the years, our church had become very involved in planting new churches throughout Ohio. And I knew from firsthand experience that new church planting remains the single most effective way of reaching people with the good news of Jesus Christ. So after praying, seeking wise counsel, and talking with the elders of RiverTree, I accepted the call to lead Stadia. For the next two years, I served as both senior pastor at our church and president of this growing church-planting ministry.

The even more amazing part of the story is that before I became president of Stadia, God was working upstream when Stadia began to ask a question: "If new church planting is the single most effective way of reaching people with the good news of Jesus and 85 percent of those who decide to follow Jesus do so between the ages of four and fourteen, what if we combined these efforts?" In 2010 the Stadia partnership with Compassion International began.

Compassion is committed to working through the local church. While this is a great strength, it is also one of their greatest challenges. In many communities of the world where poverty is at its worst, no local churches exist. Without a local church, Compassion could not start a new ministry to children. That's where our partnership met a common need. In the partnership model, Stadia starts by working with indigenous church planters to launch new churches in their home countries. As the church is launching, Compassion comes alongside the church and begins new ministries to children in the community as well. When you visit one of these new churches, you will never find Compassion or Stadia painted on any sign or church building at the new location. The ministry is marked as a ministry of that local church. It's an incredibly effective way of starting a new church and helping it to begin with a positive witness to the community.

Our partnership launched in Latin America, and today there are new churches where no churches previously existed. It's not unusual to find several hundred children at the opening day of the new church, ready to be sponsored and cared for by partners in the United States. This partnership has led to exponential kingdom growth. Since this partnership began in 2010, more than ninety new churches have been planted and nearly twenty thousand children have been sponsored!

It is clear, when you see the smiles on children's faces and find new families attending church on Sunday mornings, that these ministries are a blessing to developing countries in God's kingdom economy. But that's not the only reason I'm excited about what is happening. We found that when churches in the United States commit to plant a new church and sponsor children in these developing countries, dramatic transformation takes place in the US churches.

What Have We Seen?

First, the value of children is raised. Church leaders find that where it was once difficult to recruit volunteers and get people excited about the children's ministries, now people are interested. They're involved. Many churches find that the "generosity temperature" is raised in the church. Parents and caregivers begin investing more in their own children. Financially supporting children leads people to grow in their joy in giving and they begin to give to other ministries as well. And children become more active in God's global movement.

Our hope in writing this book is to share what we believe is God's vision for our generation: to make sure that every child has a church. For this to become a reality, it will take churches all over the world planting churches and ministering to children. Stadia's partnership with Compassion is just the beginning. When a church is captured by God's love for children and takes action, we begin to see visible evidence that God is on the move, changing lives.

Through all of this, my life has been dramatically changed. After seeing the powerful impact of this partnership, I made the gut-wrenching decision to step down as senior pastor at RiverTree and move full-time into my role with Stadia. I have no regrets! My vision is to see millions more in heaven by reaching as many people as possible in the most effective way possible with the good news of Jesus Christ. I think I've found the way to make this happen— planting new churches that intentionally care for children.

But that isn't the whole story. I left out one of the best parts.

The Prayers of the Faithful

I mentioned earlier that this journey began when I read a book by Wess Stafford. But that's not true. Unbeknownst to me, two years before I read that book, the children's director at our church, Jamie Reese, invited three women to join her to pray on a regular basis that God would wreck my heart for children. Jamie knew that my heart was preoccupied with other things, that I saw children only as a means to an end.

Jamie never mentioned her "prayer team" to me. She never beat me up or scolded me for lacking a heart for kids. She and her team simply prayed. I finally found out about Jamie's prayer team ten years after my journey of learning about God's heart for children began.

I am grateful that God heard those prayers. As a result of the prayers of those four faithful prayer warriors, God graciously changed the trajectory of my life by wrecking my heart, by showing me that small matters to him, that children matter to him.

My life has not been the same. And my hope is that yours will not be the same, that God will wreck your heart for children too.

CHAPTER 3

Running Full Circle (Jimmy's Story)

> I believe God made me for a purpose, but he also made me fast! And when I run I feel his pleasure.
>
> —Eric Liddell

> Don't you realize that in a race everyone runs, but only one person gets the prize? So run to win! All athletes are disciplined in their training. They do it to win a prize that will fade away, but we do it for an eternal prize.
>
> —1 Corinthians 9:24–25

I stepped down from the platform. I had officially just accepted my role as the fifth president in Compassion International's sixty-year history. It was a big night for the ministry. A big night for me. And a big night for my family. They surrounded me in front of the stage while the music faded and the auditorium emptied. I shared hugs with my wife, daughters, son, and son-in-law. Waiting for me were my mom and dad.

Mom looked at me, and I could tell there was a lot going on inside. She stood in front of me, not moving or saying anything. "Mom, are you okay?"

She tried to speak. There were no words. Instead, she leaned forward and gave me a hug. Mom pulled away and tried to speak again. Whatever was trying to bubble up from deep inside wasn't getting past her throat. She hugged me again.

She tried a third time but realized it wasn't going to happen—not here, not now. She leaned in and whispered my given name in my ear, *"Santiago, hablemos mas tarde."* We'll talk later.

I know my mom. I knew that whatever she wanted to tell me was going to be important. She had grown up in poverty and, over the course of her lifetime, navigated a path from poverty to provision, never losing perspective along the way.

I can't say the same for me.

A Global Childhood

I grew up in eighteen different places spread across seven countries, primarily in Latin America. My dad was an engineer, and he invested his life in bringing water, electricity, and critical infrastructure to developing countries. Mom ran our home and cared for their children. Wherever we lived, Mom kept us involved in various ways to serve the poor in our neighborhood. She never forgot the circumstances she had been raised in, living in poverty. And her concern for the poor marked our entire family in significant ways.

When I was seven, we were living in Bolivia, and after dinner we often went where everyone went—to the central plaza in downtown Santa Cruz. The square would be packed with families and street vendors and boys who would rush up to offer a shoe shine for a few pesos. But in addition to the vendors and the things to buy, there were the very poor. Every time we visited the plaza, I noticed the homeless and the beggars who lived on the streets.

On one visit, as we walked through the square, a hand reached up to me. I'd never seen a man without legs before, and I wasn't prepared to see him there, held hostage by the sidewalk. I can still remember his rugged hand reaching up to me. His pants were dirty, his empty pant legs folded underneath him. There were broken pieces of rubber under him as well, protecting his shortened limbs from the concrete sidewalk. A worn look of helplessness was on his face. Seeing him there unbolted my sense of innocence. My mind was flooded with questions. How did he lose his legs? Why wasn't anyone helping him? Everyone just walked by . . . it hurt me on the inside.

I ran to my father. "Dad, I need all the change in your pocket. That man needs it more than we do." I emptied Dad's pocket and filled the man's dirty hand. It didn't feel like much, but it was something. It was the best I could do.

Another time, a woman was spreading cardboard on the ground while her children watched her. For the first time, it dawned on me that after our walk, we had a home to return to. I would sleep in my home, in my own bed. We'd close the door and be safe. But here was a mother with children, and she was stretching out a "cardboard bed" on the sidewalk. They weren't going anywhere. This was it.

I remember thinking, "That's not fair. That's not right. Why them? Why not me?" As I grew older, my mother helped me to understand poverty and plenty. No matter what country we lived in, no matter how safe or dangerous the neighborhood, Mom took us to church. Church was the place where she ministered to the poor and distributed comfort. We weren't rich, but we weren't destitute. Mom made sure that we gave what we had to meet the needs of those who needed help. She placed herself and her children right in the middle of those needs.

One day I found my parents' checkbook. I was curious, so I leafed through the register. I saw that it was filled with the same entries, month after month after month. The same recipients. The same faithful amounts. One for the church. One for my mother's parents. One for the parents of my father. When I asked my parents about it, my father explained, "We don't own anything. God is the owner of everything. Our job is to be a steward of the resources God sends our way." I learned from my parents what it means to trust in God's provision and our responsibility to share what we have with others in need.

I saw my parents' love and concern for the poor shine through in other ways. Every church we attended benefited from my parents' generosity. I saw concrete floors. New tile and new kitchens. The churches we attended always looked a little better because my parents had been there and had shared their money and gifts with the church. In Nicaragua, there was a garbage dump at the front door of our church. My mom felt that it "wasn't proper," so she paid for trucks to come and haul away the garbage. My parents also paid to fence in the area, put in a brick courtyard, add some lights, and paint soccer lines so it was a place for kids to gather and play. I was very proud of my parents for the work they did.

My mom had the gift of giving. She never kept the poor at a distance. As I got to know some of the people and the families she cared for, I learned that poverty was fickle. It was unfair. And those truths messed with my heart.

We continued to move from country to country. I entered high school in Panama. My focus subtly shifted from the needs of those in poverty around me to the needs I felt. I had a single dream—the only place I wanted to be. The United States. I was a US citizen. Mom and Dad were US citizens, and my dad was a Korean War vet. As a teenager, I believed that the place to be was America. The USA was "Disneyland" to me. It was a place of potential, the place I wanted to call home. I had goals I wanted to achieve in the one

place where achievement counted. While it was great to be successful in the Third World, I had an insatiable hunger to achieve where
achievement counted most: in the United States.

The "First World"—a Promised Land

In the middle of my junior year, we moved to Dallas. It felt like I
had died and gone to heaven. There were malls, multilane freeways,
safe and clean neighborhoods. I started attending a great school and
took my studies seriously. I loved track and field, and I attacked
competition with a fury. My childhood in the developing world was
beginning to fade, and a new history was about to be written.

But I soon learned hard lessons of adapting to a new culture. I
didn't know what I didn't know. I didn't know, for instance, what
roll call would be like in an American school. Class after class, my
teachers would get to me and stumble. "Santiago . . ." Long pause.
"Humbierto?" A longer pause. "Is it Melado? Meyado?" I felt like
an immigrant, not a citizen.

Though my given name is Santiago, I was Jimmy to my
friends. Mom spoke Spanish, so that's the language we used at
home with her. I knew that my skin was darker than that of many
of my blond-haired, blue-eyed, all-American friends from school.
I wanted nothing more than to fit in, to be like everyone else.
But I knew I was different. I vividly remember one day when our
track team bused to a meet and we passed a police car. One of
my teammates yelled out, "Jimmy, hide! Hide! There's a cop, and
you don't have your green card!" Others joined him. "Get down!
Jimmy, get down!"

I laughed, but I wasn't sure why. I was so naïve. I had no idea
what a green card was. So when I got home, I asked my parents.
Their explanation broke my heart. All my life I had felt like an

outsider in the developing world: an American living in the Third World. Now I felt like a foreigner in America.

I coped by focusing on proving that I belonged. Since Americans value achievement, I wanted to win in the system and master the art of success. I became the classic overachiever. I hammered my studies to get straight A's. I trained harder and ran longer. I honed my skills in the high jump, hurdles, and all the decathlon events. By the time I finished high school, I had amassed awards, honors, and a scholarship offer to Southern Methodist University (SMU) and acceptance letters from West Point and the Air Force Academy. I entered the college of engineering at SMU and relished my scholarship in track and field. All the hard work, all the self-discipline was paying off. I wasn't shy about my faith either. I had not forgotten my love for Jesus and the things I had learned as a child. In fact, my quest for success was tightly woven with my faith in Jesus. My teammates knew me as a hard worker, a goal setter, and a Christian.

My senior year at SMU, I was at a meet at the University of Houston. I finished the first event, the 100 meters, and was off to a promising start on the two-day decathlon competition. I readied myself for the long jump. Taking a deep breath, I looked down, let my arms hang, and psyched myself for the leap ahead. I looked up, drew another deep breath, and raced the ever-accelerating eighteen strides of my approach run. I hit the board at maximum speed, planting my foot hard to launch toward the pit—and felt a searing stab of pain behind my knee. I immediately knew that I couldn't land on my injured leg, so at the end of my flight, I landed with all my weight and momentum on the other leg. The impact of landing on one leg twisted it, and I crumpled into the sand. I didn't know which leg to grab first.

My meet was over. I soon learned that I had partially torn a tendon, and though I was out of commission, the dream was not over. My hard work and achievement had brought me this far. It was a temporary setback. I let the twisted knee heal while physical therapy strengthened the other. My coach watched my progress. I believed I was doing better than I actually was. About five weeks later, I felt I was ready to train at full speed. Training for the pole vault, halfway down the track, I ripped the tendon again. I'd come back too soon, and my tendon betrayed me.

A few days later, the coach called me into his office. He told me to take a seat. His tone was sincere but serious. "Jimmy, I know your faith in God," he said. "It's impacted me and it's impacted your teammates."

I appreciated the compliment.

"In light of that, Jimmy, I have one question for you: Given your commitment to God, how could he let this happen to you?"

I didn't know what to say. "Coach, I don't know. I can't answer that. All I know is that faith isn't faith if you only have it in good times."

"Jimmy, the trainers have looked at your leg, and they tell me that your tendon will always be a weak spot for you. I'm afraid you're always going to be injury prone. As you know, we only have a few scholarships available. We need them for athletes who can score points at a national level. We've given you four years, but we just can't do the fifth year. I need to let you know that we aren't going to offer you a scholarship for track next year."

I was stunned. I left his office and went to the one place I knew I could be alone. I trudged to a seat at the top of the football stadium. My college track career was over. My scholarship was gone, and that meant I had no way to pay for my classes in the fall. I felt like I'd been fired from my very first job. Tears ran down my face.

I needed a miracle. I began to reason with the miraculous in mind. If the coach knew I was a Christian, this would be the perfect opportunity to prove God's love and existence. If he wondered how God could let this happen to me, would he not be impressed if he saw God heal me? I wanted everything back to the way it had been, back to normal, because normal meant competing. Normal meant achieving.

Right there in the stadium, I prayed that God would heal my leg. I even laid hands on my own knee. I was certain I was healed. To prove my faith, I walked down the steps, jumped on the track, and broke into a run. I tore the tendon again . . . for the third time.

I limped to the infield more injured in my spirit than crippled in my leg. But both were hurting. For the first time in my life, I knew that my walk with Jesus wasn't going to be a ticket to prosperity. I realized that working hard and following Jesus don't come with a guarantee of success.

My track career was over.

Moving On

I graduated with my undergraduate degree and took a job at an engineering firm in Chicago. I married my beautiful and talented wife, Leanne. The competitive spirit to achieve that drove me in school and in sports now drove me in my career. We started our home and settled into living a prosperous American life. My childhood in those Third World countries felt far away. Then a letter arrived at my home. The postmark was from El Salvador—from the world I left behind.

It read: "Santiago, I am the president of the track and field federation of El Salvador. I would like to talk with you about competing for El Salvador in the Pan American Games—and perhaps in the 1988 Olympic Games in Seoul."

Running Full Circle (Jimmy's Story)

Suddenly, it all flooded back. I felt that desire to compete. I remembered the rush of adrenaline. I longed for the opportunity to challenge myself against the best. I had unfinished business.

But there were a few problems. First, the invitation was coming from a place I'd left behind. El Salvador was in my rearview mirror, and my future in America now filled my view. Second, I knew that if I tried running, there was a strong likelihood I'd injure myself again. Still, I decided that I needed to give it a shot. I accepted the offer.

For nine months, I trained for the 1987 Pan American Games. Despite injuring my leg yet again, during the eighth event, I managed to hang on to fourth place behind two Americans and a Canadian. My showing was strong enough, and I was offered the opportunity to compete for one of the six spots to represent El Salvador in the 1988 Olympic Games in Seoul. I was all in, ready to give it my best shot. Leanne and I left Chicago so I could train in Dallas. In fact, I was heading back to SMU to train under my former coach.

The decathlon in Seoul was like nothing I'd ever experienced before. It pushed the needle on my competition meter all the way to the right. I was standing on the field of the largest and most sophisticated athletic venue I'd ever seen. Surges of adrenaline coursed through my body.

Of the ten events I competed in, the most dramatic moment happened during the high jump on the first day of competition. I was facing the reigning world champion, Olympic champion, and world record holder. I readied myself to jump—all five feet, eight inches of me. The bar rested at six feet, nine inches. The world champion had missed twice. I had missed once.

I looked at the bar. It towered above me. I glanced at the roof of the stadium. It redefined my perception of high. My eyes bounced back and forth between the roof and the bar, and strangely, the contrast made the bar look achievable. The stadium rooftop was ridiculously high, but this bar . . . it was doable. I raced for the launch point and lifted myself up just enough to clear the bar. Leaping to my feet, arms raised in the air, I ran out of the pit. At this point, if the reigning champion cleared the bar, it would be raised yet again. If he missed, the win was mine.

I sat down on the infield, waiting and watching as he lifted off for his third attempt. He rose into the air . . . and knocked the bar from its place. I had beaten the world's best, and done so wearing the blue and white of El Salvador.

I'm still stunned at how strange and impossible all of this was. Had I not injured my leg, had I not lost my track and field scholarship, it's likely that Seoul never would have happened. Truth be told, the odds of me making the US Olympic team would have been slim at best. It was only through the grace of God and an unexpected opportunity from El Salvador, my birthplace, that I was able to compete in the Olympics.

I knew that God was up to something.

The Realities of Acts 2

In addition to the thrill of competing in the Olympics, I experienced several profound spiritual moments in Seoul. At the start of the games, the pastor of one of the largest churches in South Korea offered a prayer for competitors who gathered with him in the Olympic Village. I learned that his church had 500,000 members. I was stunned. It was inconceivable to me that a single church could have that many people. I wanted to learn more about this movement, so my wife and I attended worship in an auditorium that seated 26,000. We sat in the English-speakers section and listened through headsets. When the pastor called for the church to pray, it was as if a wind whooshed through the building as people stood and their chair seats flipped back. Each believer began to pray aloud. I was surrounded by thousands of Christians thanking and praising God in an audible concert that only God could absorb.

We stayed for lunch and a presentation on the history of the church in South Korea. I learned that God was still on the move in that part of the world and saw firsthand what could happen when the local church worked well. Prayer was the foundation of it all. In the decades since the Korean War, Christians had established a concerted discipline of prayer that ensured that petitions were continually brought to God, twenty-four hours a day, seven days a week. They unceasingly prayed for God to visit and heal their land. People came to prayer sites in the early hours of the morning.

And God showed up. The church members regularly shared stories of miracles and healings and amazing relational dynamics. The only context I had for these stories and experiences was the biblical account of the explosion of the earliest church in Acts 2. As I thought about what was happening there, I realized that South Korea was an "Acts 2 experience." This 500,000-member congregation was just one expression of a countrywide renewal. In fact, at one point in the 1980s, at the peak of the movement, the number of people committing their lives to Jesus was greater than the number of babies born in South Korea each year. I saw all of this and knew that I wanted more. I wanted to be a part of something extraordinary that God was doing through his church.

Five months later, I returned to my engineering job and our small church in Chicago and took on the responsibility of leading our youth group. One Wednesday evening, I was asked to represent our church's youth group program at another Chicago church. I remember that it was a miserable night for a conference. The roads were icy and the wind chill hit a historic subzero low. As I inched my car toward the church, I remember thinking that my little church would have hammered the phone tree to cancel services on a night like this. Yet the auditorium was packed. Thousands of people were arriving. I sat in my seat and marveled at the crowd and the clouds of steam rising as people walked through the doors, packing into the auditorium. These folks were committed, regardless of the weather or personal inconvenience.

The church was Willow Creek Community Church. It felt to me that the same Holy Spirit I had seen at work in Korea was here, alive and moving in Chicago.

Again, I sensed that God was up to something.

Studies at Harvard

Shortly after my visit to Willow Creek, my father convinced me to continue with my education. I wasn't so sure. Achievement was still important to me, but I was growing more alive to the Lord and to the idea that I might give my life to a church as vital and explosive as those I had seen in South Korea and at Willow Creek. But I wanted to honor my dad, so I agreed to fill out one application. It was for Harvard. Go big or go home, I thought. You can imagine how shocked my wife, Leanne, and I were when my application was accepted. We began making preparations for Boston.

At Harvard I found that the writings of nonprofit management guru Peter Drucker were beginning to have an impact. Drucker stressed that for-profit firms could learn from the nonprofit world, and he pointed, of all places, to Willow Creek Community Church as a worthy model of study. My Harvard MBA prof was intrigued by Drucker's ideas, but he also knew that a study of management style in an evangelical church might be pushing the boundaries of acceptable academic study a bit too far for a place like Harvard. He came up with a brilliant solution. He created a class of one—me. Together, we undertook a study of church models in the US and performed an in-depth case study of Willow Creek Community Church. We looked at its leadership philosophy and the people the church was seeking to reach. For the next few months, I visited, interviewed, researched, and documented the move of God through Willow Creek. I developed a deep research relationship with the senior pastor, Bill Hybels, and his leadership team. We completed the case study and were humbled at the impact the study produced. It became one of Harvard's more profound business studies, receiving multiple updates and reprints over the years.

No matter where I went, I felt as if I was running into powerful expressions of the kingdom of God. I learned mercy and compassion from my mom in Latin America. Competing in the Olympics had given me a chance to see the work of God exploding in the South Korean church. And now a Jewish professor had set me on a course of study of the God-birthed awakening I had seen at Willow. Each of these experiences was shaping my future and transforming my life.

With my MBA finished, I accepted a job with Amoco and moved to Houston with my wife. Soon afterward, I returned to Chicago to visit Willow Creek to attend a church conference and meet with Bill Hybels to review the recently completed Harvard study. After meeting with Bill, I stood to leave. Bill took the study from me, laid it down, and walked around the desk to stand next to me.

"Oil, huh?"

I took the question as an expression of interest in my future career plans. But before I could utter a word, Bill said, "Why don't you do something really significant with your life?"

He told me about a new venture he had just launched called the Willow Creek Association. The idea was to create a support organization that would enable churches around the world to reach their full potential for the kingdom of God. I could sense my excitement growing as he talked.

Then he said something that sealed the deal for me and Leanne. He spoke about creating "Acts 2 churches." Then he asked if I would join the fledgling team at the WCA.

Leanne immediately saw the vision for this, and in 1992 I became employee number six of the Willow Creek Association. By the end of the next year, I was leading the organization as its president. It was a humbling, thrilling, and amazing place for a "third world to first world" pilgrim to land.

Have you ever felt truly at home in your calling? Have you ever needed to remind yourself that your circumstances couldn't be any better? If so, then you understand how I felt for twenty-one years at the Willow Creek Association. Everything I did, every investment of time and energy into growing effective Jesus-following churches, met the deepest desires of my heart. During my tenure at the association, God expanded my vision from the United States to a global perspective on the church. Little did I know that all of this was preparation for the next season of my life, when I would return to my roots as a child—by connecting the resources of God's people with some of the neediest children around the world.

The seeds were planted early in my time at the WCA. I remember attending a gathering of leaders in Colorado Springs, and in God's providence I roomed with Wess Stafford, who was the president of Compassion International. When the day's activities ended, Wess and I would spend our evenings and early-morning hours dreaming about potential in the church and how to increase the church's ministry to the poor and to children. Wess and I were kindred spirits, and we began a relationship that spanned over two decades. At the time, I couldn't imagine that our friendship would lead to something more. But God knew what he was doing.

The Napkin

It was the fall of 2012. Leanne and I were sitting in a restaurant with two of our most trusted friends. Everybody at the table was of the same mind. Except me.

Several months earlier, my friend Wess Stafford had announced that he was retiring. Compassion International was searching for a new leader, and while I had agreed to go through the interview process, my heart wasn't in it. I was still "all in" with the Willow Creek Association. Our vision was to create thriving churches around the world, and we still had a long way to go. The job wasn't done. I felt I had to see it through, to finish the race.

My friends didn't agree. They knew of my love for the church and the loyalty I felt to the ministry I had led for twenty years. But they also knew my story. They knew of my childhood and my quest to find success in the first world. They saw the unique ways God had been preparing me for a new role and a new calling in life. They could see how God was at work, orchestrating events behind the scenes. They could see how this new role with Compassion was a perfect fit for me, the next step in God's calling for my life.

They could see it. I couldn't. I promised to pray about it and think it through.

Those weeks of wrestling with the idea of leaving the association had been arduous. My wife had reminded me that the work we do and the callings we accept are part of the journey, not the destination. She said that if I was going to be obedient to God, I needed to look beyond what I could see for my life, what I could accomplish and achieve, to what God was orchestrating. I was beginning to see that this wasn't about the next achievement, the next big thing for me. It was about stepping into something God had planned and accomplished.

A trusted adviser had already spoken truth to me about my life as he looked over the things I had worked so hard to accomplish. "It's exhausting," he said, "to look at all your accomplishments and to think about what it took to achieve a lot of this stuff. Now that you're an adult, if you could go back and talk to yourself at eight years old, what would you tell that little boy?"

It was a great question. I thought about the places I had lived as a child among the poor in Latin America. I thought about my darker skin and my attempts to prove my worth to those who underestimated my abilities. I thought about my parents and their amazing example of compassion and selfless giving. I realized that I'd spent my entire life working hard for the next success, the next achievement. And I knew that I didn't need any of it. I slowly and emotionally choked out my answer.

"I would say to that little boy, 'Enough. Get in touch with enough. You don't need Harvard. You don't need Willow Creek. You don't need the Olympics. You don't need any of that to live out your calling to be a kingdom bringer to the max for God. You've got to get in touch with having enough.'"

Today, I can see what eluded me for so many years as a follower of Christ. My greatest kingdom contribution is not found in my achievements, even if they are done in the name of God. The greatest work in my life is the work that God, by his grace, is doing in me. It's in the kind of person he is making me to be. I realized that I didn't need to accumulate more material things. I didn't need to add another star to my resume. I didn't need to be the one who accomplished great things for God. In my case, dying to "enough" wasn't dying to material things. I was dying to "enough achievement."

My friends that day at lunch were telling me to move on, and I suddenly realized that I'd been blinded by my need to achieve for myself. God was taking me back to my roots, reminding me that I was a global citizen, not just an American. God was calling me back to love the poor, to remember the heart stirrings of my childhood. And my experience helped me to see the difference between feeling compassion and sensitivity *to* the poor and *directly serving* the poor. Best of all, God was calling me to serve the world's neediest children through the church. In many ways, it was the perfect fit for my background, my passions, my gifts, and my abilities.

My best friends could see this. I was blind. "Jimmy," one said to me, "I don't understand why this is a hard decision for you. I look at your life, and this is a total no-brainer fit."

At one point, the other friend took her napkin, grabbed her pen, and drew a large X with a line next to it. "I'm not leaving this lunch until your name is on this napkin and you take that next step in your life and make the move," she said.

I knew I wasn't getting out of there without a commitment. I signed the napkin and decided to see what God had in mind.

The Rest of the Conversation

I started this chapter by telling you about the night I was installed as the head of Compassion International. My mother, unable to say what she wanted to tell me, went home that night, and we met the next day. I asked her, "What was that all about? What was going on inside of you last night?"

She said she was proud of me. She was proud of the honor shown to me, that people trusted me to care for these children. She saw how my life experiences were coming together. But most of all, she told me how humbled she was to see how God had used her—her background and experiences growing up in poverty—to shape my life to this end. "I grew up poor," she said. "You know that. No one growing up in poverty ever thinks it will benefit their children. I never imagined that my poverty could actually play such a significant role in your calling."

Mom was right. Both of us recognized that God had used her spiritual DNA to serve the least and that it had been implanted in my life as well. "God has given us millions of children, Santiago. We need to take care of them."

And we are.

CHAPTER 4

Jesus Started Small

We must not measure greatness from the mansion
down, but from the manger up.

—Jesse Jackson

It has long been an axiom of mine that the little
things are infinitely the most important.

—Arthur Conan Doyle

It's a hard world for little things.

—Davis Grubb

He was born in a small town. He lived with a small amount of earthly resources. He performed his first miracle at a small wedding. He discipled a small group of friends. He preached in a small, unimportant region of the Roman Empire.

In many ways, the ministry of Jesus was marked by its seeming insignificance. Jesus spent most of his life in relative obscurity. Compared to the crowds that filled coliseums or the massive armies that changed the destinies of nations, the teaching ministry of this unknown Jewish rabbi seems, well, rather "small."

Jesus didn't spend his time trying to attract crowds or appeal to the rich and powerful. Jesus engaged with children at a time when children were considered unimportant and insignificant. Children were considered "small matters." He lifted children up as an example of what it means to be a disciple of God's ways. His ministry transformed the lives of children. In his preaching and teaching, Jesus told parables that spoke of the growth of God's kingdom, how God uses the tiny and small to effect massive global transformation. God's kingdom is like a mustard seed—the smallest of seeds. And to enter that kingdom, one must become like a child—the smallest of people. The way of Jesus is the way of humility, a witness to the power of God to use what we humans consider "small" to show his power and glory.

The ministry of Jesus reminds us that small matters! To change history, God loves to use the small things in this world, things that are weak and insignificant and ignored by or unknown to those in power.

When we look at the life of Jesus, what we see is the perfect reflection and representation of the heart of God. So when we look at how Jesus valued children, what we are also viewing is the living revelation of how God values children.

When Jesus arrived, as recorded in our New Testament, it was simply the culmination of the story that God began in the Old Testament.

What God Reveals through Abraham and Isaac

Let's turn to one of our favorite stories in the Bible—the story of Abraham and Isaac, an account that seems to contradict the heart of God when it comes to valuing children. I mean what kind of God—who cares about children—would ask a dad to sacrifice his son?

When Abram was ninety-nine years old, the LORD appeared to him and said, "I am El-Shaddai—'God Almighty.' Serve me faithfully and live a blameless life. I will make a covenant with you, by which I will guarantee to give you countless descendants."

At this, Abram fell face down on the ground. Then God said to him, "This is my covenant with you: I will make you the father of a multitude of nations! What's more, I am changing your name. It will no longer be Abram. Instead, you will be called Abraham, for you will be the father of many nations. I will make you extremely fruitful. Your descendants will become many nations, and kings will be among them!"

—Genesis 17:1–6

At this point Abraham is ninety-nine years old and Sarah is ninety. What is their response? Genesis 17:17 and 18:12 tell us that Abraham and Sarah laugh!

As Max Lucado writes, Sarah will be going to the grocery store to buy strained peas for the entire family because no one in the house has any teeth. Sarah will have diapers in her grocery cart for her baby *and* for her husband. Definitely a laughable situation. Further in the story . . .

The LORD kept his word and did for Sarah exactly what he had promised. She became pregnant, and she gave birth to a son for Abraham in his old age. This happened at just the time God had said it would. And Abraham named their son Isaac. Eight days after Isaac was born, Abraham circumcised him as God had commanded. Abraham was 100 years old when Isaac was born.

And Sarah declared, "God has brought me laughter. All who hear about this will laugh with me. Who would have

said to Abraham that Sarah would nurse a baby? Yet I have
given Abraham a son in his old age!"

—Genesis 21:1–7

Both of Greg's children have meaningful names. Tabitha, as
described in Acts 9, was a doer of good deeds who helped the poor.
Elijah John recalls an amazing commitment to God in preaching
the gospel. For Jimmy, his son David is named after a king who
was a man after God's own heart. Elisabeth was a faithful servant
of God and mother of John the Baptist. And Ester means "star"
who saved God's people. Even though the Spanish spellings were
chosen, they were named for the character of their namesakes.

Abraham and Sarah gave their son a name with meaning as
well. Isaac means "laughter." Every time Sarah called her son's
name, she remembered God's faithfulness.

"Isaac," (laughter) "wake up."

"Isaac," (laughter) "shut the door when you go outside."

"Isaac," (chuckle) "you're just like your father—put the toilet
seat down."

Sarah understood that her child was an incredible blessing
from God, and each time she called his name, she couldn't help but
laugh at the wonder of it all. Sarah and Abraham's life together was
filled with laughter because of the joy of sharing it with their child.

But here's where the story appears to turn dark.

Some time later, God tested Abraham's faith. "Abraham!"
God called.

"Yes," he replied. "Here I am."

"Take your son, your only son—yes, Isaac, whom
you love so much—and go to the land of Moriah. Go and

sacrifice him as a burnt offering on one of the mountains, which I will show you."

—Genesis 22:1–2

This sounds brutal—and it is—but child sacrifice was very common amid the pagan tribes where Abraham was living. The Ammonites and Canaanites worshiped a false god named Molech. They would regularly offer their children to be burned in fire to obtain Molech's blessing. Molech worship and child sacrifice took place in the Hinnom valley near Jerusalem, a valley that Jesus would later associate with hell. It would have been normal in that culture for Abraham to sacrifice his son to receive the blessing of a pagan god. But it was not normal for the living God to ask his followers to sacrifice one of their children.

Child sacrifice sounds ridiculously obscene to us in our modern context. The idea of sacrificing our children to a false god is absurd. And yet . . . sometimes . . .

We lay our children on the sacrificial altar of our careers.

We lay our children on the sacrificial altar of our broken marriages.

We lay our children on the sacrificial altar of our pursuit of more stuff.

We lay our children on the sacrificial altar of venerating a sports star more than a schoolteacher.

We lay our children on the sacrificial altar of caring more about being on the golf course than being in church as a family.

We lay our children on the sacrificial altar today to receive the blessings of the gods we worship.

Which is one of the main points of the story of Abraham and Isaac—child sacrifice must come to an end!

The next morning Abraham got up early. He saddled his donkey and took two of his servants with him, along with his son, Isaac. Then he chopped wood for a fire for a burnt offering and set out for the place God had told him about. On the third day of their journey, Abraham looked up and saw the place in the distance. "Stay here with the donkey," Abraham told the servants. "The boy and I will travel a little farther. We will worship there, and then we will come right back."

So Abraham placed the wood for the burnt offering on Isaac's shoulders, while he himself carried the fire and the knife. As the two of them walked on together, Isaac turned to Abraham and said, "Father?"

"Yes, my son?" Abraham replied.

"We have the fire and the wood," the boy said, "but where is the sheep for the burnt offering?"

"God will provide a sheep for the burnt offering, my son," Abraham answered. And they both walked on together.

When they arrived at the place where God had told him to go, Abraham built an altar and arranged the wood on it. Then he tied his son, Isaac, and laid him on the altar on top of the wood. And Abraham picked up the knife to kill his son as a sacrifice.

—Genesis 22:3–10

Now, as Søren Kierkegaard writes, if Abraham did not have a mature faith in God, at this point he could have taken matters into his own hands. He could have raised the knife and plunged it into his own chest. And everyone, like us, who would one day be told about or read about this father's great love and sacrifice for his son, would applaud his behavior. This seems like what a God who cares for children would desire. But Abraham, because he trusts God, has every intention of plunging the knife into the heart of his son. He doesn't understand *why* God is asking this of him, but he has faith that God is good and has the power to raise his son back to life. He knows that God will not abandon his promises—that his line through Isaac will multiply—but he has no idea how God will make that happen. It's an act of trust. An act of faith.

And at the very last moment, God intervenes.

> At that moment the angel of the LORD called to him from heaven, "Abraham! Abraham!"
>
> "Yes," Abraham replied. "Here I am!"
>
> "Don't lay a hand on the boy!" the angel said. "Do not hurt him in any way, for now I know that you truly fear God. You have not withheld from me even your son, your only son."
>
> —*Genesis 22:11–12*

This is a very important moment in God's history with his followers. God wants us to trust him like Abraham trusted him. To believe that no matter what happens, he will be faithful to his promises. And he wants us to be different from the culture that surrounds us.

The truth is that God detests child sacrifice. In fact, throughout the entire Old Testament, God continually upholds the value of children. Children matter to God. They hold a special place in his heart.

God's Heart for Children

We see God's heart for children as we walk through the rest of the Old Testament. Passage after passage speaks of God's concern for the fatherless and the orphan.

- "He defends the cause of the fatherless and the widow, and loves the foreigner residing among you, giving them food and clothing" (Deut. 10:18 NIV).

- "Do not take advantage of the widow or the fatherless. If you do and they cry out to me, I will certainly hear their cry" (Ex. 22:22–23 NIV).

- "But you, God, see the trouble of the afflicted; you consider their grief and take it in hand. The victims commit themselves to you; you are the helper of the fatherless" (Ps. 10:14 NIV).

- "Father to the fatherless, defender of widows—this is God, whose dwelling is holy" (Ps. 68:5).

- "Please stand up for the poor, help the children of the needy" (Ps. 72:4 MSG).

God cares for the child who has no one. He is a "father to the fatherless," an amazing promise that tells us that God sees children as his own. And God expects his followers to care for children as he does. In passage after passage, we are told to defend children, to care for them, to not take advantage of them, to help them in their need.

Children are people of significance. They play an important role in God's plans. In fact, in perhaps the most important event in world history, children played a very special role, one that you might not have considered before.

Enter Jesus, on a Not-So-Silent Night

At Christmas, many of us set up nativity scenes. We place the baby Jesus with Joseph and Mary and typically include at least one or two shepherd figures. Usually those shepherds are adult males. Occasionally there might be a younger boy.

Greg has twice traveled to Israel—to walk where Jesus walked. To ask local experts what life would have been like when Jesus was born, grew up, and lived on this earth as a man. One of the most fascinating facts Greg learned is that in the hills around Bethlehem, the adult shepherds almost never watched their flocks in the fields at night. Do you know who had that job? Their children. Their young boys and girls.

Why is this significant? Because in all likelihood, the angels announced the birth of the Savior of the world to a group of young boys and girls.

Take a moment to consider the story of David from the Old Testament. One of the prophecies about the Messiah—about Jesus—was that he would come from the house and lineage of David. But before David became king, what was he? A shepherd. When the prophet Samuel went to anoint the new king of Israel, where was David? He was out tending the sheep. The Bible tells us that he was the youngest, *just a boy*. As a young boy, he was responsible for caring for the sheep. You can read about this in 1 Samuel.

Why does this matter? It is significant that when God chose someone to be king of his people, he chose a young boy whose only accomplishment was caring for and protecting the family's sheep. When God announced the birth of the Savior, there is a good chance that he gave that announcement to children.

But that's not all. This story gets even more interesting when we dig deeper into what Bethlehem and the surrounding area were like when Jesus was born. The king at that time was Herod, and he had built a palace less than four miles from Bethlehem, where Jesus was born. The palace, named after him, was called the Herodium.

It was an amazing structure, forty-five feet high. Herod had it built on the highest hill and even had a nearby hill lowered so his residence could be seen from every direction for miles and miles. Herod's family residence was on the top floor. You can see the ruins of the Herodium today. Herod had one of the largest pools of the ancient world—10 feet deep, 140 feet long, and 200 feet wide. Herod even had hot and cold baths in his palace.

We don't know exactly where the shepherds were on that first Christmas, but in all probability the shepherds would have passed the luxurious residence of King Herod as they walked into Bethlehem to find King Jesus. Do you see the irony of this?

Jesus is small, a tiny baby born in a cold barn, lying in a manger. Up on the mountaintop sits Herod. Perhaps he was sitting in his hot bath overlooking Bethlehem at that moment. The reigning king bathes in a tub of luxury while the King of Kings lies in a bed of straw. The response of the young shepherds to the birth of Jesus is in stark contrast to the response of King Herod, the ruler of Judea. He is threatened by the baby. When Herod finally hears about the birth of this new king, he orders the slaughter of all baby boys two years old and younger in an attempt to hold on to his power (Matt. 2:16). The child in Bethlehem had willingly surrendered his power and privilege to serve all in need of rescue.

Jesus, in his adult ministry, highlights the value of children, even using them as an example of humility, as the type of person God invites into his kingdom.

Like a Little Child

Jesus values children. To fully appreciate the radical nature of his teaching about children, it helps to have some understanding of the cultural background and how children were viewed during the time of Jesus. In Roman culture, a Roman father had absolute power within his family. At birth a father could decide whether to raise a child or kill it. If he decided to kill the child, it would be left on the garbage dump outside the city. Because daughters were seen as less valuable and a financial drain on the family, it was especially common for girl babies to be discarded, left out in the night at the mercy of the elements and wild animals. In most of the world at the time of Jesus, children had little value or worth.

While Jewish culture placed greater value on the sanctity of human life, Jewish children were still considered rather insignificant, better off unseen and unheard. In fact, until the age of six, when they were deemed worthy of teaching, children were expected to stay out of sight.

But that's not what we find with Jesus. In the gospel of Matthew we read:

> About that time the disciples came to Jesus and asked, "Who is greatest in the Kingdom of Heaven?"
>
> Jesus called a little child to him and put the child among them. Then he said, "I tell you the truth, unless you turn from your sins and become like little children, you will never get into the Kingdom of Heaven. So anyone who becomes as humble as this little child is the greatest in the Kingdom of Heaven."
>
> —*Matthew 18:1–4*

Typically, a Jewish rabbi wouldn't take notice of a child before the age of six. So when Jesus answers the disciples as they are arguing about who is greatest in God's kingdom by taking a little child and telling them to act like this one, it must be a shock. Here are the mature, adult disciples of Jesus, arguing with each other, and

Jesus tells them to stop arguing and start acting like a child. It's an ironic moment, as Jesus elevates a child as an example of what it means to follow God! Jesus continues his teaching:

> And anyone who welcomes a little child like this on my behalf is welcoming me. But if you cause one of these little ones who trusts in me to fall into sin, it would be better for you to have a large millstone tied around your neck and be drowned in the depths of the sea.
>
> —*Matthew 18:5–6*

Jesus uses vivid imagery here, some of his harshest words recorded in Scripture. We don't see millstones much anymore, but these were large, heavy stones. Today you might tell someone, "Jump in a lake with a school bus tied around your neck." This is serious retribution. Jesus is telling his followers: Don't mess with the kids. They are mine. Not only are children a model for being a follower of God, they are people of value to God. Jesus warns:

> How terrible it will be for anyone who causes others to sin. Temptation to do wrong is inevitable, but how terrible it will be for the person who does the tempting. So if your hand or foot causes you to sin, cut it off and throw it away. It is better to enter heaven crippled or lame than to be thrown into the unquenchable fire with both of your hands and feet. And if your eye causes you to sin, gouge it out and throw it away. It is better to enter heaven half blind than to have two eyes and be thrown into hell.
>
> —*Matthew 18:7–9 NLT 1996*

Jesus is on a bit of a tear here. He's got everyone's attention.

Beware that you don't despise a single one of these little ones. For I tell you that in heaven their angels are always in the presence of my heavenly Father.

If a shepherd has one hundred sheep, and one wanders away and is lost, what will he do? Won't he leave the ninety-nine others and go out into the hills to search for the lost one? And if he finds it, he will surely rejoice over it more than over the ninety-nine that didn't wander away! In the same way, it is not my heavenly Father's will that even one of these little ones should perish.

—Matthew 18:10–14 NLT 1996

Let's take a closer look at this passage, beginning with verses 12 and 13. Why? Because these verses may be one of the most misapplied passages in the entire Bible. Here they are again:

If a shepherd has one hundred sheep, and one wanders away and is lost, what will he do? Won't he leave the ninety-nine others and go out into the hills to search for the lost one? And if he finds it, he will surely rejoice over it more than over the ninety-nine that didn't wander away!

—Matthew 18:12–13 NLT 1996

Most people assume this passage is about evangelism. Or they apply Jesus' teaching to those who wander away from the church, to prodigals coming back home. But notice the context. That was not all that Jesus was talking about. Look again at verse 14.

In the same way, it is not my heavenly Father's will that even one of these little ones should perish.

—Matthew 18:14 NLT 1996

As he directs his disciples' attention to a little child, Jesus is also comparing God's concern for lost sheep with the child he holds in his arms. And just like the lost sheep is at risk, isolated from the others and in great danger, children are also at risk. Like lost sheep, they are at risk when there is no one to care for them, no one to go looking for them. And like that one lost sheep, God doesn't want even one child to perish.

What Does This Mean for Us?

If you are a parent, you love your kids. And most of us have no problem caring about the children in our family, church, and neighborhood. But Jesus doesn't want us just to care about those who are close to us. He doesn't say, "Hey, be concerned only about the kids in your own home. Be concerned only about the kids who make good grades. Be concerned only about the kids who are soccer stars. Be concerned only about kids who are in your own school district." When Jesus talks about going out to seek the lost sheep, we need to think about all those who are lost and need help. We need to think about children who are at risk. We need to track down the child who is wandering, who is scared, who is alone. Jesus is telling us that God cares about *every* child. He wants us to look for those who don't have someone to love them, someone who cares for them. No matter how far out on the margins a child is, God says, "I care about that one."

Yes, God cares. But the real question is, do you care?

Do you?

Welcoming Jesus

Consider what Jesus says in verse 5: "And anyone who welcomes a little child like this on my behalf is welcoming me" (Matt. 18:5). Jesus is challenging his followers to welcome one another, using a little child to illustrate his point. He is giving us a challenge to be a welcoming community, to be compassionate and caring to those in need.

And who is in greater need than a child at risk? When we care for a child at risk, we're caring for Jesus! A child without a home . . . that's homeless Jesus. A child going to bed hungry . . . that's starving Jesus. A child who's lonely . . . that's lonely Jesus. A child who's being abused . . . that's Jesus being abused. A child who's being shipped around from home to home . . . that's Jesus being shipped around from home to home. A child who has no place to go for Thanksgiving . . . that's Jesus with no place to go for Thanksgiving. God loves the helpless and the weak. He loves those who need his help. And he places great value on children. For Jesus, small matters. He wants us to care for children—those in our families and neighborhoods and communities—and the child at risk, the child in need—anywhere in the world.

Greg was awakened one night by the buzzing of his cell phone on the floor by his bed. Because the phone buzzed persistently, Greg reluctantly slid out from beneath the covers to see who could be sending such an urgent message. The screen read: "Amber alert! Nine-year-old girl abducted in Warren, OH. Red Ford Mustang with black stripe."

Greg was sickened by the message but quickly climbed back into bed to try to slumber again. He did say a quick prayer for the little girl before beginning to count sheep. Greg was a long distance from Warren, and he didn't know anyone who drove a red Ford

Mustang. It was the middle of the night . . . what in the world could he do?

Then he thought, What if it were my little girl who was abducted? I would scream through the Amber Alert, "Please get out of your bed! Have you seen my little girl? Get in your cars and drive until we find the red Mustang. If you can't go out, please spend the night on your knees in prayer. This is my little girl! My little girl is lost! I am begging you! Please help me find her! Please help to bring her home!"

That is the way God feels about every child on this planet. "Please help me find my child who is lost. Please pray for the little ones who are far away from home. Please join me in searching for every one of my children who is separated from me. Please help me bring them home. Please help me."

It's the heart of God for children. It's the heart of Jesus for children. It must be our heart for children. Because small matters.

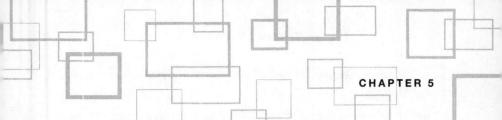

CHAPTER 5

What Love Does

For Christ's love compels us.

—2 Corinthians 5:14 NIV

We are blessed for one reason and one reason only . . . to be a blessing to others.

—RiverTree Christian Church

Why do we do the things we do? What governs our actions and choices? There's probably no single answer to those questions. Sometimes we do the right thing because we know we should. We ought to behave or act in a certain way because we were taught, "It's the right thing to do." We are motivated by external factors like respect for authority or fear of punishment. We act because there is a reward, pleasure, a benefit. We know that a certain choice will produce good results.

Sometimes we do things because we want to benefit somebody else. Their welfare—maybe even their survival—might be at stake. Many would say this is a higher motivation because somebody else gets the benefit. We won't benefit directly from what we do. Our actions are focused on the other person, doing what is best for them.

Yet even when we are "others focused," there is often a hidden gift, an unheralded outcome that surprises us. Do good to others, do it repeatedly, do it over the long haul and it produces personal transformation. When we serve others and sacrifice for their good, we don't end up being the same as we were when we started.

If you are a parent, think back to those days—or more accurately the nights—of parenting your newborn child. When parents put their baby down after his 10:00 p.m. feeding, they are longing for the time when their little one will finally sleep through the night. But they know that it's not going to happen tonight. They know they'll be awakened again at 1:30 a.m. And again at 3:15. Perhaps again at 5:20, all to meet the needs of a hungry baby. Parents choreograph an elaborate dance, taking turns to visit the nursery. In all of this, there is no glory. There's more selflessness here than there is glory. The parents are giving more than they receive. It's more about sleepy responsibility than wide-eyed zeal. They sacrifice the luxury of uninterrupted sleep, knowing the routine will be the same again tomorrow night.

And yet, in all of this sacrifice, something is happening beyond caring for the immediate needs of the infant in their arms. They begin to experience a bonding and love for their child that's so deep, they can't imagine being anyplace else. In the quiet and the dark of the early-morning hours, a transformation occurs. They look at this helpless child and experience the joy of selfless love, of stepping outside themselves to fully meet the needs of another person. Over time, this selfless giving creates an even deeper identity as a parent, a willingness to give whatever they have and to do whatever it takes to give their child the love they need. Fiercely protective, intensely loyal, and hugely nurturing, parents are changed as they care for their little ones. They are transformed.

This is the hidden irony of love. It is the unheralded outcome of giving that is focused on others. We never go into it with our own benefit in mind, but in saving others, we save ourselves.

Love Transforms

When Greg and his wife, Julie, brought their adopted son, Elijah, home, they were joyfully inundated with family and friends. As the loving well-wishers met Elijah, the most common phrase the family heard was, "He is so blessed. Imagine what his life would have been like if you had not adopted him." It was a compliment. It was their way of sincerely honoring this beautiful commitment to a new child. But what many did not understand—what even Greg and Julie weren't aware of at the time—was that Elijah's presence in the family would be a blessing for them as well. The blessings are numerous. Because of Elijah, the family has a deeper understanding of God's "adoptive" love for them. Because of Elijah, who is black, the family is more aware of racial segregation and prejudice. Because of Elijah, the family has an entirely new network of friends—other families who have adopted children. Elijah's presence in the family has expanded their awareness of God's presence and helped them to more fully understand what it means to love others as God has loved them. If Greg and Julie had never adopted their son, they would not have known these blessings. And while this wasn't their motive for adopting, they're both hugely thankful for what they've seen and experienced. Countless adoptive families echo the same gratitude.

You may have heard the story of Sean and Leigh Anne Tuohy. If their names don't ring a bell, you may know them from the movie *The Blind Side*. Sean and Leigh Anne are the adoptive parents of NFL football star Michael Oher. The Tuohys brought Michael into their home when he was sixteen. He had no family to care for him and was living in poverty. Michael was adopted by the Tuohys and lived with them until he started college at the University of Mississippi, Ole Miss.

Leigh Anne and Sean believe that what they learned about giving and sharing their love with Michael transformed them. Before Michael, the Tuohys did not spend time sitting together or eating meals together. All of that changed when Michael joined the family. Michael became a loving brother to their biological son and daughter, and even though there were challenges, the Tuohys say that their lives are far better now than they would have been without Michael. Leigh Anne said, "Most people believe that Sean and I saved Michael, but the truth is, Michael saved us."

Loving others and giving ourselves for the sake of others transforms us.

The Reason We Minister

Those who lead in the church or in the community have a special privilege and role to play in inspiring others to love and serve children. But there is a daggerlike question that cuts to the heart of our motivations, one we as leaders must ask ourselves. We can believe to our core that we are transformed when serving children. We may know that serving children can be a healing experience. We may agree that serving children helps us to better understand the love of our heavenly Father and what it means to be his children, his disciples. All of this may be true. But these are secondary benefits. We are not motivated to serve because it is an opportunity for self-improvement or education. We do not serve as a means to grow our ministry. Do you care for children? If so, why? Press yourself on this one. Why do you care for children?

As Greg explained earlier, he came face-to-face with his own motivations when he realized he was using children to accomplish his own purposes, his own goal. His experience is not unique. Most pastors are concerned about growing their church, about their

Sunday-morning message. It's go-time! They are *on*, and all aspects of the ministry—from greeters to the teaching of the Word—become critical. For many pastors, the children's program is important because it provides a convenient service for the adults. Many pastors will agree that adults are more likely to come a church that provides a welcoming place for their family. They are looking for family activities. They want to know their children are safe. They want to know there are excellent age-appropriate programs for each one of their kids. That's a key reason why many churches invest and labor to offer the best programs for young children and teens. Maybe that's one of the reasons why your church invests in ministry to children.

These are all good things. We should do our best to provide good programs and activities for families. We should have clean and safe places for children. Ministry to children is a great way to reach their parents. But is that the primary reason why we love and serve children? Is children's ministry just a bridging strategy to reach adults, a means to an end? Ask yourself these questions: Do you see a child's decision to commit to God to be as significant as an adult's? Are the budgets for child and youth programs equal to the value of a child in the kingdom of God? These are questions that should challenge leaders and shape the way they create a church that reflects the heart of Jesus toward children.

Children cannot be a means to an end. While it is wonderful to see parents attend a church because we serve their children, what matters most is that our perspective on children is transformed. We must learn that children are not a "small matter" in God's purposes and plans. Children are not a small matter to the kingdom of God. Instead, we must learn that *small* matters to God. God values each child as a unique person, created in his image. Each child is someone Christ died for, someone who needs to hear the message of the gospel, who needs our care and compassion, who needs our resources, our time, and our attention. To serve children, our values, our priorities, and our hearts need to be changed from the inside out.

We have found that when new churches are planted, the ones that have a strategic plan to care for children and prioritize ministry to children are much more effective, much more likely to succeed. But our motivation to care for children cannot be to grow a large church. It cannot be to have a successful new church plant. Our hearts must be set on caring for children simply because God cares for children. Children have inherent value in and of themselves.

No Small Matters of the Heart

So how does this concern for and valuing of children become one of the core values of our lives? Is it a matter of obedience? Yes. Or is it a matter of the heart? We say yes again.

James, one of the leaders of the early church and the half brother of Jesus, writes in his letter to the church: "Religion that God our Father accepts as pure and faultless is this: to look after orphans and widows in their distress and to keep oneself from being polluted by the world" (James 1:27 NIV). Read that again. Is James giving us a command here, or is something else going on?

James is specifying certain actions to the church, actions that are descriptive of a quality faith. Followers of Jesus will do these things. Among all the things a Christian can do, he is naming these as activities that are acceptable and faultless. These are things we can do. And if you aren't doing them, you can start doing them. James is looking at the heart *and* at our obedience. He is both describing and prescribing here. He is giving marching orders. He is also describing the character and outcome of a God-shaped life. It is both a portrait and a command.

For some people, a passion for children will come from a moment of heartbreak. A visit to the developing world will unravel the tightly wound cocoon of plenty in which we raise our children. It will birth a passion to care for a child at risk through sponsorship or other ongoing support that emphasizes child development. For others, encountering children with special needs will pierce their heart and lead them into service opportunities in their own cities. Others will coach, mentor, teach Sunday school, or be the destination home on the block where kids go for fun and to feel safe. Having a heartbreaking experience is one way that God can stir up your passions and engage your will to serve kids.

But what if you are reading this and you are thinking, "I haven't had an experience like you are describing. My heart has not been broken for children"? What if children aren't a passion for you or for your church leadership? If that's true, we would encourage you to wrestle with what the Scriptures teach and to lean into obedience. Obeying God's command to care for children can lead to long-term heart transformation. God validates his priorities in the Word as you walk in obedience, making his priorities your priorities as a leader.

Work That Carries the Kingdom (Jimmy)

I have learned most of what I know about obedience through the discipline of training. As you can guess from my life story, some of this was birthed in athletics. Let's define training as the disciplined, consistent leaning into rhythms and repeated practices to develop skills and abilities that become second nature. Is that really any different from a long view of obedience?

I remember my days of pre-Olympic training. I had left my job, and Leanne and I were living in Arlington, Texas. My days were defined by diet, exercise, and constant repetitions of the decathlon events. It sounds like a life of privilege, and in some sense it was. But it was also one of the hardest things I've ever done. Nothing brought dread to my days like training for the 400-meter event. To prepare, my regimen called for all-out, full-speed 500-meter sprints. I ran as fast as I could for nearly a third of a mile. I'd check my time, catch my breath, and do it again. And again.

I had an affectionate name for days like this. I called them my "throw-up days." During one particular session, I was about to start my workout. I was alone, no coach at my side. I sat on the track and stretched, but my thoughts sprinted down a decidedly depressing lane: "You're going to throw up after this. What's the point? You're not going to medal. You don't know if your tendon will hold out. You left your job, and you're not earning any money. You're wasting your time. What the heck are you doing?"

I took off my shoes, flung them across the track, and sat there.

Over time, other thoughts battled back: "You're going to quit? You're done? Really? You've got unfinished business with the Olympics, and you're just going to walk away?"

I sat there for about half an hour.

More thoughts. "You've been dreaming and training to go to the Olympics your whole life, and now you have a chance to go. You don't have a guarantee, but this is your only shot."

That was enough to make me stand up, put on my spikes, run my 500s—and throw up.

We all know that nothing good ever happens without effort. It takes profuse spiritual sweat to enter a life of spiritual training that creates the heart of Jesus in us more strongly each year. We are convinced of this spiritual truth: If you make a significant move to follow Jesus in exalting children in your life and in your church, there will be "throw-up days." It will be real work.

But if your motivation is wanting the kingdom of heaven to reside in you and his will to be done on earth through you, then you can expect to see God, through your church, meet the critical needs of children living in prosperity and children living in poverty. The kingdom of God removes needs through others-focused living. And you can be a part of it. We are carriers of the kingdom of God.

You might recall the story of Elisabeth, the girl my daughter Bizzy sponsored in Guatemala. When we left that story in chapter 1, Elisabeth's mother had died and her father was living far away to work and support the family. She and her siblings had been taken from their home and placed in an institution, and they desperately needed help. In the end, help came from Elisabeth's church—the church where her Compassion child development center was located. The people in her church recognized Elisabeth's and her family's needs. The pastor and another church in the community offered to help.

They joined Elisabeth's father in a hearing before a judge to plead the case for keeping this battered family together. The court had three conditions: Elisabeth and her siblings needed a daily guardian for the periods when their father was working in Mexico; someone would need to provide a secure one-room home constructed with cinder blocks rather than the tin-and-wood shanty the family now occupied; and a concrete floor was mandated for safety and sanitation.

This was more than Elisabeth's father could muster, but not more than God's people could provide. Together, the two churches invested the time and resources to build a cinderblock home with a secure door. A concrete floor lifted the family off the dirt. And during the court hearing, one of the women from the local church committed on the spot to become the daily guardian. God's people *worked* with discipline and faithfulness to love this family.

When my daughter Bizzy revisited Elisabeth two years later, she stepped into a secure concrete home with a chicken coop constructed on the lot. And she met the faithful saint—there's no other word to describe her—who invests her life on a daily basis as guardian to ensure the well-being of Elisabeth and her siblings.

Because of the obedient, disciplined, and consistent work of kingdom people, both Elisabeth and Bizzy have undergone massive growth in their understanding of God. They both are truly "carriers" of God's kingdom to one another and to the world.

A Transformation Reinforced by God (Greg)

When I transitioned from pastoring RiverTree to leading Stadia, the church provided a gift for my twenty-five years of service—a monetary gift. I didn't want the money to go to me, so I asked them to give it to plant a new church in Colombia. We were excited to see how the gift would be used, and it became a semiregular topic at our dinner table.

One evening I came home and found an envelope resting on my laptop. It was addressed: *For God's Churches.* I slid my finger under the flap and took out the contents. Inside was $196. It was every penny Tabitha, our fourteen-year-old daughter, had earned and saved from babysitting. I was stunned. My first thought was, "Oh, Tabs, you don't want to give *all* your money away." My second thought flowed just as quickly: "Tabs, you can ask me for anything right now, and as long as it's right and good, Daddy will do it for you. I will entrust you with so much more."

And then a third. "This is how God feels about me when I invest in things close to his heart." This was a teachable moment where God spoke to me. It was as if he was saying, "Greg, you just gave your transition gift away to something close to my heart, and now I am going to entrust you with more because I see you are trustworthy."[1]

I did not give my transition gift away expecting a wonderful spiritual lesson from the Lord. I didn't expect to get anything in return. But seeing Tabitha's gift opened my heart and my understanding to receive God's personal affirmation. We saw the same principle at work in our church. There was a time when we begged for children's workers and pleaded for volunteers. Pastors often need to sound a constant drumbeat and make platform pitches and recite bulletin announcements to recruit more children's volunteers. Then we began promoting God's vision for loving children. We gave opportunities for Compassion sponsorship of children. What happened? Almost three thousand children were sponsored, our church budget for children's ministry was covered, and we no longer had to beg and plead for children's workers.

This is the power of a God-transformed heart. Our leaders experienced God's generous supply as we gave the church God's vision for loving kids and provided them with opportunities to respond. That's the amazing thing about God's Spirit and his Word. Changed hearts produce changed behaviors in ways that guilt, nagging, and pleading never can. And even if we don't feel the passion, we can still practice obedience, allowing God to shape our hearts to align with his until they are in tune with God's priorities. As we walk in obedience, God reinforces the transformation and provides more internal and external resources to live out his kingdom values.

Keep It Small

Remember what Leigh Anne Tuohy said earlier in this chapter? "Most people believe that Sean and I saved Michael, but the truth is, Michael saved us." We see the power of this truth all the time. We are saved as we save others.

When Julie and Greg traveled with several families to Ecuador over a Thanksgiving holiday, their goal was to visit several Stadia and Compassion partner projects and serve their sponsored children. On that trip, something unseen was at work. Someone unseen. God's Spirit took those experiences and worked a transformation in the lives of those serving. A Christmas card from one of the women on the trip contained a short poem she wrote a few weeks later:

> Some don't have a house decorated with lights.
> Or a tree filled with presents and garland wound tight.
> You won't find them shopping in a local mall.
> Searching and searching for the cutest new doll.
> No purses, no shoes from a specialty store.
> Just a few little presents lay on their dirt floor.
> The kitchen isn't filled with the aroma of pies.
> No sighting of Santa will appear in the sky.
> No selfies, no snapshots to remember the fun.
> They just cherish each moment of every loved one.
> So, how did they bless us with nothing to give?
> It was the hope and the happiness in the way that they live.
> God gave us a gift and it didn't fit in a cart.
> Their smiles, their hugs, and all the love in their heart!

We serve children because it is God's work, his call upon our lives. We serve them because we love them. And we press our churches to make children a priority because children matter to God. And as we serve and sacrifice, as we shed tears and share moments of joy, God transforms our lives.

CHAPTER 6

Enough Is Enough

Enough is as good as a feast.

—Mary Poppins

O God, I beg two favors from you;
    let me have them before I die.
First, help me never to tell a lie.
    Second, give me neither poverty nor riches!
    Give me just enough to satisfy my needs.
For if I grow rich, I may deny you and say, "Who is
    the Lord?"
    And if I am too poor, I may steal and thus
        insult God's holy name.

—Proverbs 30:7–9

A man can eat only one meal at a time, wear only
one suit of clothes at a time, drive only one car at
a time. All this I have. Isn't that enough?

—Stanley Tam

Greg and Julie led a trip to Ecuador a year ago to visit several new churches. At each new Stadia church plant, more than two hundred children in the community were being supported through the ministry of the church in partnership with Compassion. Five families from our church wanted to witness the life-transforming difference when children are given the hope of Jesus and cared for by a local church. Altogether, eight parents and ten children (ages eleven through seventeen) were in the group that went to Ecuador.

The Possibilities of Enough (Greg)

We traveled in November over the Thanksgiving holiday. Not only did we as parents want to see God's amazing work, but we especially wanted our children to experience what life was like for those who have so much less, materially, than we do.

We saw thriving churches bringing hope to communities through the good news of Jesus. We saw children laughing as they learned and played in a safe environment. We saw mothers smiling as they held their babies, having been taught by volunteers from the new church how best to care for their newborns. One of the most meaningful times was when we served lunch to hundreds of children on Thanksgiving Day (in Ecuador, Thanksgiving Day is not a holiday). We gave each child a plate of rice that included chicken and fried plantains—the most nourishing meal these children would eat that week.

That evening, back at our hotel, we sat in a circle to discuss the events of the day. Everyone agreed that it was their best Thanksgiving ever. Instead of cooking and devouring our traditional holiday feast, we had served food to needy children. Instead of lying on the couch in a post-turkey daze, we had kicked soccer balls, played games, and rolled in the dirt with joy-filled little ones. Instead of praying words of thanksgiving for all we had been given throughout the year, we experienced the privilege of offering our lives as a sacrifice of thanksgiving to God. We had shown our gratitude to God by loving these children and giving our resources and time for them. And we had been blessed.

On our last night before heading home, we had a special dinner in a local restaurant. As a group we wrestled with the "so what?" of our trip. It had been a great experience, a lot of emotional moments, but we wondered, What difference would it really make in the way we lived when we returned home? What would we do differently as a result of what we had seen and done?

At the end of our meal, the teens in our group went off together in a corner of the room. After their huddle, they told us they wanted to fund a new church plant in Ecuador. Several of them had sponsored children on their own through Compassion International. They each told us, their parents, that they wanted to give their upcoming Christmas gifts away. They were clear: They already had enough. They did not need more.

I'm happy to report that our children raised the money for that new church, the church has opened, and more than two hundred children are being cared for. God worked in the hearts of our children, helping them to see that they had enough and how they could help others. They know it truly is more blessed to give than to receive.

The Poverty of Too Much

The power of living with enough is utterly life transforming. It's living in a state of contentment, knowing at a deep level that your needs are met. When we come to accept that enough is enough, that what we have is sufficient, we are freed to bless others out of our abundance. Amber Von Schooneveld writes, "There is a poverty of too little, there is also a poverty of too much."[1] And Mother Teresa, who worked and lived amid some of the deepest poverty in the world, once said, "To decide that a child must die so that you may live as you wish" is the greatest spiritual poverty.[2]

Americans pump $7 million into the US retail industry every minute. We purchase an average of 1,440 McDonald's burgers, 5,695 Starbucks drinks, and $84,000 worth of items on Amazon every sixty seconds.[3] By themselves, these facts don't mean anything. But we raise them to highlight the fact that the majority of us living in the United States have more than enough. Our purpose is not to make anyone feel guilty every time they eat a cheeseburger or consume a latte. We want to prod your heart and ask a question we all should ask ourselves on a regular basis, How much is enough? Are the choices I'm making each day good stewardship of what God has given to me? Am I consuming more than I need? Am I using resources God has given to me and depriving a child of basic human needs? Is my life consumed by the things of this world, or am I consumed by the things of God?

Here is the principle: The farther a person is from enough, the greater the *spiritual risk*. Consider a child living in extreme poverty. He can barely bring himself to even think about Jesus. His primary concern is basic survival. Where will he get his next meal? Will he be safe tonight? What will he wear for shoes? He is at risk. His needs are both material and spiritual, but his material needs take priority. They are real and urgent and they must be met.

A child living in extreme prosperity doesn't have material risks. He has food, clothing, and a place to live. He has more than he needs. He is in danger of forgetting, or never having learned, that every good thing comes from God. The abundance of his material resources can numb his sense of dependence. He can become self-reliant rather than God-reliant, self-centered rather than others-centered. It's easy for him to disregard the biblical teaching that we are blessed to be a blessing to others. He might not even know that what he has been given is meant to be used to honor God and to love others. All of this can lead to an attitude of entitlement.

Ellie and her father recently traveled to South America to visit a Compassion child development center in a local church. Ellie is sixteen. She has been sponsoring a child for more than two years. Ellie met her sponsored child and they spent the day together. Two children from two different worlds—yet both at risk.

Ellie's sponsored child, Melanie, lives without enough to meet her basic needs. Ellie has more than enough. The beauty of this relationship is not simply that Ellie meets Melanie's material needs. Their different circumstances are being used by God to draw them both toward a greater appreciation of God and his provision of their needs in Christ. Through this relationship, God meets both physical and spiritual needs, and he uses their friendship to help them each recognize their neediness and how God is enough for them. In different ways, they see the truth that the apostle Paul writes about in 2 Corinthians 8:9: "For you know the grace of our Lord Jesus Christ, that though he was rich, yet for your sake he became poor, so that you through his poverty might become rich" (NIV). Each child experiences the truth of the gospel as applied to their own circumstances and needs.

Finding Your Enough

For all who have made a commitment to follow Jesus, we have a responsibility to seek God's wisdom to determine with Jesus how much is enough. When we have an eternal perspective, we know that this world is passing away. The things we accumulate—whether they are material possessions, wealth, or worldly acclaim—will not last beyond this short life. Our lasting treasure will be reflected in what we give away, in the fruit of God's love in our lives.

So we need to look at what we have and ask ourselves some difficult questions: How many pairs of shoes are enough when others are living without them? How nice should the vehicle we drive be when others have no transportation? How many diet sodas do we need to drink when others have no clean water? How big should our house be when others do not have a roof over their heads?

There are no simple answers to these questions. Our goal is not to prescribe a legalistic list that defines what is acceptable and what is not. Yet it is equally wrong to assume that our lifestyle is fine and never think about how we spend God's resources and use the gifts he has given to us. Our cultural default is to consume without regard for the effect our consumption has on others.

Shortly after World War II, leaders of our country were trying to figure out how to boost the economy. Retail analyst Victor Lebow advised the following: "Our enormously productive economy . . . demands that we make consumption our way of life, that we convert the buying and use of goods into rituals, that we seek our spiritual satisfaction, our ego satisfaction, in consumption. . . . We need things consumed, burned up, replaced and discarded at an ever-accelerating rate."[4] The drive to seek our satisfaction in consuming material goods has been the dominant philosophy driving our economy and, ultimately, it is what drives many of our lives day to day. Here is a gut check for you to consider: Just six months after the date of purchase, only 1 percent of our stuff is still in use.[5] Is that true for you? If so, you may have fallen into the trap of consumption.

How big is this problem? We contend that the number one spiritual disease in America is consumerism. In Matthew 6:21 Jesus says, "Wherever your treasure is, there the desires of your heart will also be." So where are we putting our treasure, our financial resources and wealth? Do we use our treasure to satisfy ourselves with things we don't need or even use, or are we investing it in the lives of others, meeting their needs and serving our communities? Are we spending our treasure on things that will soon be thrown in the trash, or are we spending it on people who will last for eternity?

Maybe you've heard the phrase "planned obsolescence." Product designers today plan how quickly they can make the stuff they create go bad while still retaining the consumer's trust in their brand. But the truth is that our stuff can't go bad fast enough to keep the economic machine afloat, so there's a twist on this idea, something called "perceived obsolescence." Perceived obsolescence occurs when companies and marketers convince us that what we have, even though it still works great, is no longer any good. Typically, this is done by changing the way something looks. The heels on women's shoes go from fat to skinny or from high to low. Automobiles receive a new look every few years so that the car we drive looks out of date. A new version of the iPhone is released about every year. We throw things away that are still perfectly good.

We all fall into this trap. For most of us, we have more than enough. That iPhone from last year is still fine. Those running shoes can go another year or two. But the temptation we face is to go with the flow, to consume, to use, to replace our stuff with more stuff that's just a little bit different from what we have. Five percent of the world's population is in the US, but we consume 30 percent of the world's natural resources.[6] And our consumption of so much of the world's natural resources is driving many people in developing countries to move to cities to work in factories in substandard conditions. Many live in slums; some even live in garbage dumps. Every day, each individual in America produces 4.5 pounds of garbage. That's 1,642.5 pounds of garbage per year, per person.[7] It is time for us to say enough is enough. And that's where we need help, for it is only in tandem with Jesus that we can determine what's enough.

Enough Will Vary

We'll say this at the outset so it is clear: We cannot determine how much is enough for another person. In fact, we should accept that someone else's enough probably will be different from our enough. You may determine that a late-model Toyota Camry is enough for you to drive, while another person may decide that a new Ford Mustang is enough for them. You may determine that a 1,600-square-foot house is enough for your family, while another person determines that a 3,600-square-foot home is enough for them. Sleeping in a tent while on vacation is enough for you, while someone else decides that staying in a four-star hotel is enough for them.

The key is to focus on our own life and to not become bitter when we see someone living with more than we have decided is enough. Begin with the realization that everything we have is a gift from God, that it all belongs to him, and that each person will be held accountable by God for how they use the gifts and resources he has given to them. Some will have more resources, wealth, and abilities than others, but it's not for us to decide how much is enough or how they should use what they have been given. We must not become self-righteous because we've decided to live with less than what others have. Our enough must flow out of a heart that is at peace with God. We are to be content with what Jesus has given us and give to others out of a heart filled with gratitude and joy. We are blessed by living with our enough because we are able to bless others with our generosity and be a part of God's work in their life, helping them find freedom from their poverty.

The Surprise of Enough (Greg)

Several years ago my wife and I were invited to have dinner with Wess Stafford, now president emeritus of Compassion International, and his wife, Donna. Wess picked us up from the airport in his late-model SUV. As he drove us to their ranch, he told us that they'd found the land for an amazingly low price. When we arrived, we discovered they lived in a simple 1,600-square-foot home. This was where they had raised their family. Donna and Wess had done much of the construction themselves.

Before dinner, Wess gave us a tour. He showed us the basement, which he had remodeled so that each of his two daughters could have her own bedroom. Though cozy, their home wasn't all that great when compared with most American homes. After dinner, we were sitting at the table discussing lifestyle choices when Wess said he would like to buy a John Deere tractor someday to farm his land.

Surprised, I said, "Wess, you lead a multimillion-dollar global organization. You can surely afford a tractor!"

His wife looked at me and said, "Greg, we work with poor children. We have enough."

That conversation was one of many that profoundly affected the way my family thinks about our money. We've learned that it helps to surround ourselves with other followers of Jesus who have made similar choices and have decided to live with enough. This isn't easy, but when you are all in it together, it's easier to give, easier to say no to more.

Enough Is Contagious

One of our friends, Mike Foster, began a ministry called The Junky Car Club. Mike is committed to driving only used vehicles that are fully paid off. Why? So he can use the money he would have paid on a car loan to give to those in need. Mike chose to direct those funds to sponsoring children through Compassion. Mike has laughingly said, "I knew that once I started this club, I would never drive a nice car again!" But Mike's leadership has been an example to others, leading thousands to make the same choice. They have chosen to live with less so that more children can be sponsored. Mike's "enough" has blessed many children living in extreme poverty around the world.

And that's just the beginning. When parents choose to live with enough, that mindset can infectiously spread to their children, inspiring them to sacrificial giving. Be intentional. Be creative. Be an example to your children and consider implementing some of these ideas in your family:

- *Teach them to give stuff away.* Talk with your kids about God's generosity and how everything we have is a gift he has given to us to be used to love others. Encourage them to think about giving away something they already own for every gift they receive at Christmas or on their birthday. Some children ask friends who come to their birthday party to bring a monetary gift to support a favorite ministry or a child they sponsor through Compassion instead of a birthday gift.

- *Talk with your children about sponsoring a child.* Help your children to learn about the children in other countries who have material needs. Teach your children that God has blessed them to be a blessing to others.

- *Expose your children to people living in poverty.* Talk with your pastor or mission team and find opportunities to serve the poor in your city or neighborhood. Consider a short-term trip. There is nothing like a short-term missions trip to help children gain a bigger picture of the world and to teach them the value of enough. You can talk about these experiences before you go and after you return to help them to understand how our resources can be used to love others.

- *Memorize Bible verses together.* Look for passages that speak of the poor or of God's generosity to us or that encourage us to love and be generous with others. For example: "If you help the poor, you are lending to the Lord—and he will repay you!" (Prov. 19:17); "Do to others whatever you would like them to do to you" (Matt. 7:12); "Give, and you will receive. Your gift will return to you in full—pressed down, shaken together to make room for more, running over, and poured into your lap. The amount you give will determine the amount you get back" (Luke 6:38).

- *Talk as a family about what is enough for your family.* Encourage your kids to think about what they *need* (to survive and thrive) versus what they *want* (things they may enjoy, but aren't essential).

- *Set an example by giving something and donating your time or money to help someone in need.* Your children are watching *you.* Actions speak louder than words.

- *Give your children experiences instead of things.* Our lives are filled with stuff, things we use for a few days, then set aside and forget. This is especially true with children's toys. Help your kids to see that memories and time spent together have value that goes far beyond having the latest video game.

- *Work through a book or curriculum as a family to help your children understand what it means to have enough and to be content, generous.* There are many great options. One suggestion is *Step into My Shoes* from Compassion International. The curriculum lets you immerse your family or small group in a four-step walk toward "living from enough." You learn from a Ugandan pastor named

Tom, his wife, Nancy, and their children. You step into their shoes and take a walk with Jesus, seeing how Scripture calls us to follow Jesus in loving God and neighbor. (For more information, visit *stepintomyshoes.or*g). Whatever you choose, make it a regular part of your family devotions. Encourage your children to ask questions and apply what they learn to their own lives.

- *Look for volunteer opportunities that are geared toward children.* Ask your pastor or your children's ministry director at your church for ways your kids can help. Older children often can work with younger kids in their classes or youth groups. Your children can serve other children in your community through mentoring, helping out in reading programs, packing lunches, filling backpacks with school supplies, etc.

Finally, as you consider different ideas, we encourage you to seek out other families who can join you in these activities. Doing these things with others not only makes it easier but also makes it fun! Hebrews 10:24 says, "Let us consider how we may spur one another on toward love and good deeds" (NIV). God loves to see his children encouraging one another in showing love and being generous toward others. Remember . . . small matters!

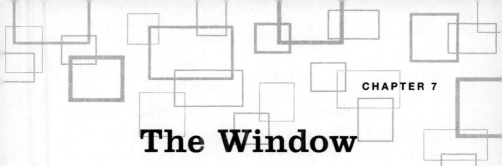

CHAPTER 7

The Window

All children are my children.

—Nana Mouskouri

Children are not a distraction from more important work. They are the most important work.

—C. S. Lewis

If I could relive my life, I would devote my entire ministry to reaching children for God!

—D. L. Moody

When you visit a Compassion child development center, it is pure spiritual adrenaline. You get countless hugs from the children. You immediately sense a tangible passion overflowing from the pastor and the center staff. There are celebrations, music, and presentations. Each of the local churches we partner with is marked by the flavors of that country, the neighborhood, and the unique personalities of the children who pack the church. One particular visit Jimmy made to a church in Nicaragua took on special meaning for him. He found himself just a few blocks from one of the neighborhoods where he grew up. These were the streets he had once explored on a little Honda 50 motorbike as an eight-year-old boy.

Usher In the Children (Jimmy)

I was sitting in the front row in the church courtyard as the program began. That's when I saw him. A cinderblock wall, about seven feet high, surrounded the courtyard, and over the top of the wall I saw a shock of dark hair and dark eyes peering over the edge. Even though I was surrounded by children, there was something about this little guy, peeking over the wall, that grabbed my heart.

It felt as if I were looking into a mirror. I could see myself as a young boy, more than four decades ago. That boy reminded me of all the times I was the outsider. In each new country we moved to, I'd start out on the outside.

From his vantage point on the outside of the wall, the boy could see the decorations and balloons strung around the courtyard. He saw the children, probably his neighbors, wearing their Compassion T-shirts and sports pants. He heard the music, the laughter, the clapping. He could feel the energy and buzz of the event.

Carlos peeking from behind the wall

The Window

I locked my eyes on this little guy and was stunned by the contrast. Here on the inside was life, vitality, safety—a sense of belonging. What little boy or girl wouldn't want that? But he was on the outside. He was working hard just to get a glimpse of what was inside, out of his reach. It wasn't right.

I leaned over to a staff member next to me and asked her if we could bring him in. She went outside and found him on a narrow tree stump, balancing precariously on his tiptoes to see over the wall. Like Zacchaeus who climbed a tree to see Jesus, this little guy wanted to see what God was up to in the church courtyard.

When he saw the worker coming in his direction, he jumped down, thinking he was in trouble for peeking over the wall. He had no idea that I wanted him to be my guest of honor. He took off, bolting down the street. I was so proud of our staff member. Instead of turning around and coming back, she followed him home. She met his mother, explained who she was and where she came from, and simply asked the little boy's mom if he could join us at the center. The worker was surprised to find out that his mom knew of the Compassion center at the church, but she didn't have all the paperwork she needed to get him registered. The worker said she'd help her take care of those details. A short time later, she ushered six-year-old Carlos, his mother, and his sister over to sit with me.

Carlos represents more than a special encounter or an emotional heart tug. In my mind, Carlos is a picture of the millions of children who are at a special stage of life. Each one has a need to be seen, pursued, and brought from the "outside in." Each one has needs to be met.

Effective Good

If you're anything like we are, you may find yourself suffering from "cause fatigue." Bring up your social-media feed and you are bombarded by evils to combat, hungry children to feed, and disasters to respond to. Visit church and you hear about needs from missionaries and opportunities to serve. Stories on the evening news grab at your heart. There is no lack of causes we're invited to join. Disasters, diseases, movements, and causes are constant because we live in a fallen world. The requests to "do good" will not go away anytime soon. We could fill our wrists and forearms with bracelets to remind us of all the worthwhile causes that are trying to alleviate life-crushing obstacles. This avalanche of needs and statistics can numb us, even inoculate us from caring. After all, how much can one person do?

Maybe we're asking the wrong question. What if the question isn't how much we can do, but where we can be effective? Part of the answer rests with the unique passion and concern for specific people that God has given us. This is where we take our cue from Jesus' own priorities. We are reminded of the unrestrained anger Jesus expressed toward anybody who would push a child away or fail to provide protection for a child. We're reminded that Jesus welcomed children. The Old Testament is filled with reminders that God has a special concern for the fatherless, for the child in need, for the child at risk. There are many great causes, but we are convinced that children are near the top of God's priority list. Children are Jesus-sized priorities. Invest in the life of a child, and the potential for effective change in the child's life is huge.

Do you know when most people decide to follow Christ? We believe the answer is not just an interesting fact but also a resounding affirmation that God loves children. We say this because the most receptive window of time for a person to accept Christ is between the ages of four and fourteen. One study concluded that 85 percent of commitments to Jesus are made in this spiritually influential season of life. This is true throughout the United States and for children around the world.

Think about your own commitment to God or the commitments made by your family and friends. While not everyone comes to Christ during these years, we've found that when we ask a gathering when they came to know Jesus, their answers validate this "4–14 window." One of Greg's favorite exercises is to ask a group to raise their hands if they decided to follow Jesus between the ages of four and fourteen. Whether it's a group of five or a gathering of five thousand, the majority of hands go up.

Think of the implications. There are approximately 1.2 billion kids on the planet between the ages of four and fourteen.[1] But that number just tells us they exist. Each one is being shaped and formed by their circumstances—by their culture, by their parents or lack of parents—for good or bad, based on what investments have been made in them. These young lives are crashing onto the shore of adulthood in tidal waves. And these young adults, shaped by their circumstances, will impact the world for generations to come. We see it with our own children, with the children in our churches and neighborhoods. It's true whether a child is surrounded by plenty or by poverty. The shaping of character is a complex and delicate thing.

Recently Jimmy received a gritty, in-the-moment video captured on a mobile device from a Compassion child development center in Nicaragua. One of the children, Roberto, was in the pastor's office because he had misbehaved. He had bitten the hand of the tutor assigned to his class, hard enough to break the skin. She received medical attention, and Roberto was sent to the pastor's office. He knew he was in deep trouble. Scared and a bit defiant, the young boy listened to the pastor correct his behavior and probe for the reasons behind his attack on the tutor. Roberto's story was heartbreaking, but not all that unusual in the developing world. A mom who had died. An alcoholic father. This little guy was filled with anger, sorrow, and fear. He was lashing out with behaviors that got him into trouble.

Stop for a moment and think about Roberto's life, about this biting event and the discipline it demanded. Think about what a little boy like this, growing up in poverty, feels when his mom is ripped from his life. She's never coming home. He sees his dad drinking and drunk. What does this boy think about? How does he feel? Afraid? Sad? Does he wish he could run away? Does he wish his dad would? These are big problems for a little guy. What do you do with pain and fear like that? How do you help a young boy deal with the emotions sloshing around inside of him that he can't put into words?

It's a moment for discipline, yes. But this became a holy moment.

The pastor realized that Roberto was desperately looking for help. He knew that the boy's deepest need was to know Jesus, to know that he was loved, that he belonged. He needed to be made healthy from the inside out, to be adopted by his heavenly Father. So the pastor explained who Jesus is and what he had done. He invited Roberto to pray with him, phrase by phrase. During the prayer, the pastor realized something wonderful was happening. He accessed the video function of his phone. This is what happened next.

With a loving hand on Roberto's shoulder, the pastor led him in a prayer we fully understand. "Lord Jesus, thank you because you love me." Roberto softly echoed the words. "I need you," the pastor said.

Roberto paused. He leaned forward on the desk, buried his head in his arms, and cried the cry of a little boy who needs the God he is talking to. A little boy who needs Jesus to show up in the middle of a discipline session.

It's hard to describe what Roberto's crying sounded like. It was high-pitched. Wailing wouldn't be an overstatement. The pastor allowed the boy's tears to flow and then led him to pray for forgiveness. To pray for Jesus' presence. And to thank God for coming to him at that very moment.

The video ended there, dissolving to a new scene, recorded later when Roberto's tutor entered the office and sat next to him. She seemed a bit wary, and Roberto would not look at her. When she heard about his decision to receive Jesus, she drew him close and put her arm around him. Still visible were the massive bite marks on her fingers, slathered with purple-red antiseptic. Roberto buried his head deep into her shoulder. He sank into her hug and her tender pats of assurance.

"You know I love you," she said.

Roberto lifted his small arms and wrapped them around her neck. Imagine how secure he must have felt at that moment, being loved and nestled in arms that reminded him of his mother. Roberto's tears flowed again.

This is just one example of the work we can do in the 4–14 window, when grace makes its presence known and we dial in and focus on a boy or a girl who needs Jesus. The 4–14 window is about young people waiting to hear the gospel, waiting to be transformed by God's grace and the love and nurture of his people. For many, it is about the 400 million children in the world who live in abject poverty.[2] Sometimes it seems as if there's an agenda to array obstacles against them.

Some families are so poor, education isn't an option. They can't afford the tuition, uniforms, or shoes. Some children are forced into child labor or worse—sold into perpetual serfdom by parental debt that can never be paid. Some children are sexually exploited in their homes. Others are abducted by deviant adults. Many are caught in worldwide sex trafficking. Parents who were emotionally abused as children often continue the never-ending legacy of neglect and abuse. Fathers leave home and family, and mothers are driven into poverty. Children are cared for by aging relatives. Abject poverty, where people "live" on less than $1.25 a day, erodes the basics that a child needs to grow and mature. If these moms and dads, caregivers and guardians could fill the gaps abject poverty creates, they would. The fact is they often need help.

Now let's be clear. Those living in the United States are not the rescuers of the world. Not all children in poverty lack the love of a healthy and strong family. Many homes getting by with less have incredibly strong bonds of care and unity—stronger even than those of prosperous families living with plenty. Jimmy's mother, for instance, grew up in poverty, but she grew up with love in a home filled with dignity.

All children need the same life-giving love and compassion. They all need security. A home with loving adults. Education. Health care. A place to belong. Spiritual growth. A safe place to play. Opportunities to learn. Discipline. Relationships. Mentoring. Hope. Unleash these on a child in poverty and watch out! Watch them thrive! Not only are children who are four to fourteen receptive to learning about Jesus, they are growing in multiple areas of their lives. But don't take our word for it. Independent empirical research bears this out.

The Evidence of Effective Good

When Dr. Bruce Wydick, professor of economics and international studies at the University of San Francisco, evaluated the impact of popular strategies for helping the poor, child sponsorship received the highest rating among all of the long-term development interventions. But Dr. Wydick went even further in his research. He launched a six-nation, two-year study of adults who had participated as children in Compassion's holistic child development program between 1980 and 1992. He wanted to know how these adults benefited, if at all, from Compassion's program. For a control group, his researchers studied the life outcome data of unsponsored siblings, other children in the community who were not part of the program, and children in communities where Compassion's program wasn't available. In total, Dr. Wydick's project reviewed the adult data of 1,840 formerly sponsored Compassion children and 8,160 adults who were not involved in the program but were raised in similar circumstances. His results were published in the prestigious *Journal of Political Economy*.[3] The findings demonstrated "large and statistically significant positive impacts" on the lives of these formally sponsored Compassion children:

- Former Compassion-sponsored children stayed in school
  1 to 1.5 years longer. In the developing world, school
  attendance has been shown to have a major influence on
  one's future well-being.

- Former Compassion-sponsored children were up to
  13.3 percent more likely to complete primary school.
  Depending on the country, those who started secondary
  school were 27 to 40 percent more likely to finish. And those
  who went to university were 50 to 80 percent more likely

to complete their education. That last statistic is amazing. Granted, the percentage is large based on smaller numbers of young people who attended universities in developing countries. Nevertheless, the statistical difference is striking.

- These Compassion graduates were 14 to 18 percent more likely to hold salaried employment. They were 35 percent more likely to secure white-collar positions. Many were better equipped to pursue service-oriented professions such as teaching and nursing.

- And finally, these former Compassion-sponsored children were up to 75 percent more likely to be leaders in their communities and 70 percent more likely to become church leaders. This finding is particularly gratifying. It's only natural they would give back through church leadership, since the development program, run in partnership with a local church, provided the tools, experience, and mentoring that facilitated a significant portion of their growth.

A child of Compassion in Sri Lanka

A child of Compassion in Mexico

Add to the findings of this study some recent findings on children and church attendance in the United States:[4]

- Kids who attend church are far less likely to get divorced later in life, have better skills to overcome poverty, and do better in college than kids who do not attend church. Regular church attendance is particularly instrumental in helping young people to escape the poverty of inner-city life.

- Children's involvement in church activities is a strong predictor of academic achievement as well. Children who have greater religious socialization also have increased levels of educational attainment.

- Going to church reduces a child's likelihood of being a criminal. Students attending "weekly religious services are less likely to use drugs or alcohol, to engage in delinquent behavior, to get in trouble at school or to have poor grades when compared with their peers who attended church less than monthly or not at all." Youth who considered religion to be fairly important or very important in their lives were less likely to engage in risky behavior. For many of these youth, church attendance reinforces messages about working hard and staying out of trouble, orients youth toward a positive future, and builds a transferable skill set of commitments and routines.

We'll admit that there are no guarantees. The power of transformation comes from God working through his church. But clearly, child-development programs and church involvement have a positive effect on children living in poverty. When we talk about the 4–14 window, we have something in mind that is far more strategic than adding an item to a Christian "to do" list, something more concrete than being "for children." We believe that there are specific things we can do to make investments in the life of a child at a key period of life that will make a difference in the quality of that child's life into adulthood. We're talking about tangible grace to a child who is eager to respond. Eager to be affirmed. And eager to build a future more robust than the child's preceding generations.

We're all about full-fledged implementation of Jesus' priorities. He didn't stop at a campaign for children. He invited a child to be at his side. He hugged a little one. He exalted a child's worth.

A Respectful, Imaginative Recasting

Let's replay the scene where Jesus initiates a conversation with a Samaritan woman at a well. The conversation this woman had with Jesus was so insightful and powerful she forgot that she was a community outcast and rushed into town to tell everyone about the amazing man she had just met. And people listened! She must have been amazingly persuasive, so persuasive, in fact, that Jesus called his followers' attention to the village residents who were leaving the town and making their way toward them.

"I tell you, open your eyes and look at the fields!" Jesus said. "They are ripe for harvest" (John 4:35 NIV). One translation puts Jesus' quote this way: "Behold, I say to you, lift up your eyes and look on the fields, that they are *white* for harvest" (NASB). Some commentators have noted there aren't crops in the Middle East that are white at harvest time. The "white" may be referring to the varied hues of the light-colored tunics worn by the villagers. If so, Jesus wanted to clearly point out that human lives were the harvest. These villagers were interested. Curious. Eager to learn who this prophet was.

Here's where we want you to respectfully reimagine children walking out of the village instead of villagers. Project the image of children in poverty. Project the image of children in plenty. In either case, imagine children ripe for harvest:

- Ripe with openness.
- Ripe with hunger to be educated.
- Ripe to feed a hunger for God.
- Ripe to be mentored and shown what is true.
- Ripe with a need to be as healthy as possible.
- Ripe with a desire for friends.
- Ripe with a drive to find purpose in life.
- Ripe with freedom to have a dream.
- Ripe with openness to be affirmed in their God-based worth.

Jesus tells us that a harvest of lives is there, people who are ready for God. They are eager to hear. Ready to learn. And we can lovingly serve them on behalf of Jesus and their Father who made them. They're kids like Carlos, looking over the church courtyard wall, curious about what is happening.

Open your eyes. Kids like this are all around us. Pay attention to one of them. Run after one of them. And move one of them from the outside in.

CHAPTER 8

Caring for Children in Your Home

I have become convinced that the spiritual war occurring in individual lives is pretty much won or lost by the age of thirteen.

—George Barna

We tend to do a lot for our children but not nearly enough with our children.

—Wess Stafford

Be what you want your children to be.

—Mark Merrill

What does it take to raise healthy, stable kids? How do we navigate parenting our children from preschool to adulthood with more than just a survival mentality? As parents, Jimmy and Leanne are now on the other side of toddlerhood, grade school, and high school. The youngest Mellado child is nearly done with college. The good news is that Jimmy and Leanne are still standing. The better news is that all three of their children are standing as well—each one with their own walk with Jesus.

Few things are more powerful than watching your own kids seeking to learn what it means to follow Jesus. We hope and pray, for ourselves and our children, that each of us would lean into and live out our calling as disciples of Jesus, to increasingly bring the kingdom of heaven here on earth. *Nothing is more important.* We love the way John Ortberg refers to our role on earth as Christ followers. He calls us "kingdom bringers." And, of course, the first and ultimate kingdom bringer was Jesus. A kingdom bringer is an idea demonstrated for us at a breakfast Jesus hosted two thousand years ago.

Amazingly, even after his resurrection, Jesus was still bringing the kingdom of heaven to earth. It's in his divine DNA. After all, it's his kingdom. And on this particular morning, he is meeting his disciples on the beach and serving breakfast. Peter is there.

Peter and Jesus had some things to talk about. A few nights earlier, before he was crucified and buried, Jesus had been arrested by the religious leaders and the Roman authorities, and there, before a crowd of witnesses, Peter had denied knowing Jesus. Not just once. Three times.

Now, with the grilled fish eaten and the coals dying out, Jesus turns his attention to stoking another fire—the one in Peter's heart. "Simon son of John, do you love me more than these?"

Peter's response became public record. "Yes, Lord," he said, "you know that I love you."

That's when Jesus pointed out the true nature of love. He said, "Feed my lambs." We don't know whether Jesus let his command settle in Peter's mind or came back at him immediately, but he had his follow-up question ready to go.

Again Jesus said, "Simon son of John, do you love me?" The account doesn't tell us whether Peter was defensive, shocked, confident, or confused, but he was on the spot.

He answered, "Yes, Lord, you know that I love you."

Jesus said, "Take care of my sheep." Jesus is pressing. Love isn't just a feeling that comes and goes, a passing emotion. It isn't a declaration of loyalty. Peter lost his credibility on that matter the night Jesus was arrested. In God's economy, love is about caring for the people Jesus cares about. Jesus' next question brings this to the forefront. He wants Peter to understand that this question requires more than an answer. It requires a painful realization about the true nature of love.

Again Jesus said to him, "Simon son of John, do you love me?"

Peter was hurt because Jesus asked him the third time, "Do you love me?" He said, "Lord, you know all things; you know that I love you."

Jesus said, "Feed my sheep" (John 21:15–17 NIV).

Jesus had good reason to belabor the point. He had given Peter the call for the rest of his life—to be a fisher of men. But Peter had defaulted to his old script: a fisher of fish. In front of the young men on the beach, Jesus made it clear that his purpose for life didn't have an alternative. Jesus was straightforward. Straight up. Peter was to bring people to God and care for them spiritually—feed them with God's Word. He was a "kingdom bringer." It's as if Jesus is saying, "Care for my people, and you'll show your love for me."

As parents, grandparents, teachers, coaches, and all people who love children, our privilege and our call is to shape kingdom bringers. What does it take?

Kingdom Bringers at Home (Greg)

I was traveling in Africa about fifteen years ago, visiting missionaries who were planting a new church in Mtwara, Tanzania. One of the missionary couples there had young children. We were walking along a dusty dirt road on a 110-degree afternoon when this young missionary father asked several of us, "What do you do to disciple your children?"

Our daughter, Tabitha, was only one year old at the time. I hadn't given much thought to how I would teach her to be a follower of Jesus. I absolutely wanted her to love Jesus, but I had no plan for how to help bring this about.

As we continued up the dusty road, we tried to give wise answers to this young dad, but the truth was evident—at that point in our lives, none of us had much to offer when it came to wisdom for discipling the children living in our homes.

Today, years later, in the front of my journal, I write my "rules to live by." Rule number three for my life simply states: "The most important people I disciple are my children."[1] There will be lots of children I come in contact with over the years (and those children matter), but the most important children I disciple are the children God has entrusted to me in my own home. There are millions of children on the planet who desperately need to hear the good news of Jesus Christ (and those children matter), but the ones at home with you need to matter most to you.

There are children in your neighborhood. There are children in your school system. There are children in your church. There are children on the other side of the world. And *all* of these children matter! But the most important children you disciple are your own.

We don't want to get to heaven someday and say to God, "Look at this amazing ministry I led. Look at this church I planted. Look at this awesome church I built. Look at the orphanages we funded. Look at the children we sponsored." And have God ask us, "But where is Tabitha? Where is Elijah? Where are your own children?"

The Picture and the Prescription

When it comes to discipling our own children, we love God's instructions in Deuteronomy 6. This is a great section of the Bible. It starts with a beautiful picture of the results of a great discipling relationship and then gives the prescription for creating it.

First the description of that beautiful picture:

> These are the commands, decrees, and regulations that the LORD your God commanded me to teach you. You must obey them in the land you are about to enter and occupy, and you and your children and grandchildren must fear the LORD your God as long as you live. If you obey all his decrees and commands, you will enjoy a long life. Listen closely, Israel, and be careful to obey. Then all will go well with you, and you will have many children in the land flowing with milk and honey, just as the LORD, the God of your ancestors, promised you.
>
> —*Deuteronomy 6:1–3*

And then the prescription for creating it:

> Listen, O Israel! The LORD is our God, the LORD alone. And you must love the LORD your God with all your heart, all your soul, and all your strength. And you must commit yourselves wholeheartedly to these commands that I am giving you today. Repeat them again and again to your children. Talk about them when you are at home and when you are on the road, when you are going to bed and when you are getting up. Tie them to your hands and wear them on your forehead as reminders. Write them on the doorposts of your house and on your gates.
>
> —*Deuteronomy 6:4–9*

We love the picture: a good relationship with God, enjoyment of a long life, all going well in a land flowing with milk and honey! But how do we get there? Let's dig deeper into Deuteronomy 6:4–9—those prescription verses.

> Listen, O Israel! The LORD is our God, the LORD alone.
>
> *—Deuteronomy 6:4*

Adults, God is talking to us here. We set the example. In 1 Corinthians 11:1, the apostle Paul says, "Follow my example, as I follow the example of Christ" (NIV). So who or what is your "god"? Is it your career? Your money? Sports? Recreation? Do you know how you can know who or what your god is? Take a look at your calendar. Look at your bank statement. In what or in whom do you invest most of your time? Where do you place your most valuable resources? Our children are watching us, and they know what we treasure, what's most important to us.

What does God say is most important in life? Well, we know the answer because Jesus was asked this very question. A guy comes up to Jesus and he says something like, "Hey, Jesus, what matters most in life?" (Mark 12:28–31). And Jesus answers, "Whoever wins the NCAA football championship."

No. Jesus told him that what matters most is loving God and loving people. What matters most in life are your relationships. First is your relationship with God, and out of the overflow of that relationship, we love others. A rich, meaningful relationship with God will empower deep, meaningful relationships with other people. So who or what is your god? If we want to disciple our children, it starts with us saying, "God, you are my God, and you alone are my God."

Back to Deuteronomy 6.

And you must love the LORD your God with all your heart, all your soul, and all your strength. And *you* must commit yourselves wholeheartedly to these commands that I am giving you today.

—Deuteronomy 6:5–6, emphasis added

Again, it starts with you as a parent. You've heard the phrase "The apple doesn't fall far from the tree." It all begins with us as parents—we are that tree!

It's amazing to see this play out when you read the Bible, especially in the Old Testament books of 1 and 2 Kings and 1 and 2 Chronicles. We will read that a king was a good king, and his son, just like his dad, was a good king. Or it will say a king was a bad king, and when his son became king, he too was a bad king, just like his dad. Or it will say that the new king was a wonderful king who followed in the goodness of his mother. Or a king was one of the worst ever because he followed the evil example his mother set for him.

God gives parents incredible responsibility and power in raising their kids. The most important people we disciple are our children, and it all begins with the example we set for them.

You must commit yourselves wholeheartedly to these commands that I am giving you today. Repeat them again and again to your children. Talk about them when you are at home and when you are on the road, when you are going to bed and when you are getting up.

—Deuteronomy 6:6–7

We need to capture teachable moments. We love the story about the dad who captured a teachable moment with his elementary school children. The family rule was that his kids were not allowed to watch a movie that had a PG-13 rating or higher. All three of his kids came to him begging him to let them see a PG-13 movie that was playing at the local cinema. The movie was a blockbuster, and many of their friends had gone to see it. "No way," Dad said.

The kids didn't give up. After talking to several of their friends who had seen the movie, they made a list of the movie's pros and cons.

The cons:

1. There's swearing in the movie, but only three words.
2. The only violence was a building exploding. ("And you see that on TV all the time," they said.)
3. And finally, you didn't actually see the couple in the movie having sex—it was just implied, off camera.

The pros:

1. It's a very popular movie. If they didn't see it, they would feel left out.
2. The movie contained a good story and plot. There were some fantastic special effects.
3. Many members of their church had seen it and said it wasn't "that bad."

The kids wanted their dad to reconsider. The dad said he wanted to think about it for one day. The next day, his kids were excited. "We've got him. He's got to let us go." Their dad called them into the living room. He had made a fresh plate of brownies. They looked and smelled delicious.

Dad explained to his kids that he had seriously considered their request and decided that if they would eat one of the brownies, he would let them go to the movie. But, like the movie, there were pros and cons to the brownies. The pros:

1. They were double-chocolate fudge.
2. They had caramel drizzled over the top.
3. They were still warm.

The cons . . . just one: Dad had included a special ingredient. The brownies contained just a little bit of dog poo. He had mixed the dough well. They probably wouldn't even be aware that they were eating dog poo. Therefore, if any of his children could stand to eat a brownie that included just a little bit of poo, then he would let them see the movie that included just a little bit of poo!

As parents, we know there will be times when we have to deal with the impurities that are all around us in life. We can't protect our children from being exposed to the evils around us. We walk with our kids through difficult situations, taking advantage of teachable moments so they will be prepared to live on their own as followers of Jesus. Our goal is not to take our children out of the world, but rather to equip them to live as kingdom bringers in this world. Some situations we help our children avoid. We use other situations to teach and train.

Teachable moments are all around us. Pray for safety when you're in your SUV, getting ready to go on a long trip. When you see the colors of the leaves changing, take a moment to point out how creative God is. Sponsor a child and teach your own children about the needs of others. Help plant a new church to teach your children how much God loves all people. Teachable moments can be minor or monumental.

In Deuteronomy 6:8–9 is God's command to "tie [the commandments] to your hands and wear them on your forehead as reminders. Write them on the doorposts of your house and on your gates." God wants his teaching—his Word—to be all around us. To be an integral part of daily life. He is reminding us to be intentional about discipling our children and teaching them how to be "kingdom bringers."

REI

Here's a great tool that we both use to disciple our kids. It's the acronym REI. It stands for

Relationships
Experiences
Information

Yes, we know that REI is also an incredible outdoor adventure store. That helps us to remember that the Christian life is meant to be lived as an adventure. Here is what the R, E, and I of intentional discipleship represent:

1. Relationships

In one minute, list five relationships God has used to influence your life for him. Play the *Jeopardy* theme song in your head or hum it. Either mentally or on a scratch pad, make a list of those people God has used in your life to help you better follow Jesus. Start now.

Our guess is that you quickly came up with five names, and you probably could have listed several more. That's because relationships matter. The same is true for our children. As their parent, you are the most influential relationship in your child's life. Are there others? The popular African proverb says that "it takes a village" to raise a child. We believe it takes a community of believers to disciple our children. We seek out relationships with other families, adults, children, and singles who can help instill biblical values in our children. We want to expose our children to people who are actively growing in their faith and seeking to follow Jesus. We covenant with close friends on this matter, agreeing to pour our lives into one another's children. The Bible teaches:

- "Bad company corrupts good character" (1 Cor. 15:33).
- "Become wise by walking with the wise; hang out with fools and watch your life fall to pieces" (Prov. 13:20 MSG).

We believe in surrounding children with good company and wise people to walk with.

It Takes a Team (Jimmy)

As intentional as Leanne and I try to be in our walk with Jesus, we're not the "be-all and end-all" source of influence in our children's lives. Raising healthy kids is a community responsibility shared inside the local church. Our small group became that trusted wider sphere of child-shaping influence that invested a God-oriented view of life in our children.

This was a small group who walked together through twenty years of parenting and raising our kids in community. We journeyed through the crossroads of truth and life in all its messiness and imperfections. Our parenting mistakes taught us even more than the sermons we heard or the classes we attended. Leanne and I don't know how we would have survived without this safe place where we could talk and be real. This was a grace-filled group, free from agendas other than the simple goal of helping each other and helping our kids grow to maturity in Christ.

Part of the group's success was the commitment we made. We were purposeful in giving each other the access and privilege to influence and speak into the lives of each other's children. I remember when one of the kids was asking questions about college and wondering where to go. We took his concerns as seriously as if he were one of our own children. We created a huge chart that listed all the pros and cons by category. Other times we spoke into the lives of the kids on issues like drinking, pornography, dating, grades, and sports. We covered everything, avoiding nothing. Having other adults investing in our children was invaluable. My child may tune out what I have to say as a parent, but when another adult says the same thing, their ears suddenly open up!

Leanne and I treasure the legacy of our small group community. It was like twenty years of Amish barn raising with the choice lumber of young lives. Where else on the planet can you find relationships like these?

2. Experiences

Let's repeat the same exercise we did with relationships. In one minute, list five experiences that God has used in your life to help you be more like Jesus. Start the *Jeopardy* theme song now and make your list.

Our guess is that some of you had an easier time making this list than you did your list of relationships. Experiences are another profound influence on our lives. Bob Goff, in his wondrous book *Love Does*, recounts several amazing stories of adventurous experiences with his family. Experiences where his family learned together. Experiences where his family served together. Experiences where his family showed God's love to others.[2] If someone were to write a book about the experiences of your family, how extraordinary would they be? Would your family experiences reflect your desire to help your children to more fully follow Jesus? We have found that one of the most powerful discipleship experiences we can offer our children is that of serving together. Baking cookies and delivering them to the widow who lives down the street. Going to an assisted-living center during the Christmas season and throwing a birthday party for Jesus. Preparing and delivering Thanksgiving meals to those living in poverty in our city. Raking leaves for the elderly. Anything we can do to show the love of Jesus to those around us.

One of our best experiences has been serving on missions trips together. My (Greg) daughter, Tabitha, has been on three trips to South America with me. We visited church plants and walked through communities ravaged by extreme poverty. We ate in homes with dirt floors and barely a roof. We played with children who were absolutely delighted to have *gringos* embarrass themselves while playing their national pastime (soccer) with them. The result? At sixteen, Tabitha now sponsors two children and earns the money to pay the monthly sponsorship fee. She prays for the children daily and writes to them regularly.

Greg's daughter, Tabitha, with her sponsored
child Naedelyn in Ecuador

Investing in Experiences (Jimmy)

I'm amazed when I hear what it costs to raise a child in today's economy. Government studies and private research groups have calculated that by the time a child born today finishes a state university, you'll drop a tidy $512,044.[3] That's clothes. Cars. Food. Child care. Toys. Mobile devices. You name it. Perhaps that's part of the problem.

While every parent wants to provide a good quality of life for their children, there is tremendous pressure on families today to keep their children equipped with the latest and greatest. Some parents fear that their children will fall behind or will not be prepared for the changing economy. But we must not forget that children need far more than material assets. They need extraordinary experiences. This is how kingdom builders are developed.

In the Mellado household, we evaluated the experiences and opportunities available to our children in various ways. For example, we had a category labeled "non-miss opportunities." These included camps and retreats, but there were several other experiences we wanted for them as well. We wanted our children to see that the world around them is filled with people in need, with families and children living in poverty. And we wanted them to experience interacting with children and families in need.

My mother grew up in poverty, and even though she eventually escaped it, she made a point of keeping the plight of the poor before us, wherever we lived. I remember how, as a child, I saw a homeless family preparing to sleep on the sidewalk or the man with no legs begging for money. At a young age, I understood that life was difficult and that most people were doing their best to survive day to day. I knew this was not how it was meant to be. As I grew older, my parents taught us that being a follower of Jesus meant caring for the poor, reaching out and serving those in need. My wife and I knew that we wanted to teach our children this. But we weren't sure how to do this, raising our kids in an environment like the United States. We felt our lives in America were disconnected from how the majority of the world lived. In some ways, we were living in a bubble. Our well-resourced environment was a *liability* to engaging our kids in God's kingdom work.

We looked for opportunities to give our children extraordinary experiences that would disrupt their normal routine in unexpected ways. As our children were entering their teenage years, my dad was leading one of the largest construction projects ever undertaken by the country of Bolivia. We took our kids to visit my father there. We visited the project where he was working and saw the community where I lived as a six-year-old boy. Seeing what life was like in my old neighborhood in Bolivia helped our kids understand what I had experienced as a child. We visited a family that lived in a one-room adobe house. We asked God to give us eyes to see his work around us. Leanne and I were praying that God would use these experiences to disrupt our children's lives, hoping that God would show up in circumstances that were foreign to them.

Part of raising teens is teaching them the value of work and how to manage money. Our kids had many of the same experiences that other teens had. They worked summer jobs, learned to save and give, played sports, and hung out with their friends. But Leanne and I saved money to support them on trips to the Dominican Republic, Guatemala, El Salvador, Panama, Mexico, Zambia, and Bolivia. We (and they) would say that their lives have been deeply affected. These extraordinary experiences, exposing children to the needs of the poor and to the global church, can pay extraordinary returns that compound into eternity.

3. Information

Here's a last exercise for you. Start the *Jeopardy* theme song again and write down five sermons or Bible studies that God has used to transform your life for him. Start now.

If you are like most people we've asked over the years, you probably had a more challenging time making this list. Greg's mom has listened to him preach for twenty-five years, and she could come up with only three sermons! Our point is not that sermons or Bible studies are insignificant. Far from it. Information is important, but in our experience, it plays a supportive role, working with relationships and experiences to enable transformation. To say it another way, a hunger for information will typically flow out of our relationships and experiences.

We've seen it happen. While helping poor people, a son might ask, "Daddy, why does God let such bad things happen to these people?" This gives us an opportunity to respond with information about God's provision for us and our responsibility to provide for the needs of others. Or in the context of experiencing a beautiful hike through the hills of Pennsylvania, a high school daughter might mention that her science teacher said there is no Creator. Then we talk about God as Creator and why we believe this to be true.

Experiences place us in situations that raise questions, and these questions require answers. Experiences provide opportunities to offer information. Experiences open doors to a child's mind by creating curiosity, interest, and a desire to learn. Simply teaching facts or imparting information does not necessarily lead to life transformation.

There's no teacher like real life. But even real-life experience isn't the best teacher if it isn't accompanied by the right perspective and a change of heart that leads to a change in behavior. Moses had it right when he spoke to the people of Israel, teaching them how to impart the truth of God to their families. Moses told Israel to "impress [these commandments] on your children. Talk about them when you sit at home and when you walk along the road" (Deut. 6:7 NIV). We love this idea! What does it mean to talk about the things of God "along the road"? "Along the road" simply means taking advantage of the moment at hand. We must be attentive to our circumstances and to the hearts of our children, ready to impart information that's needed right then and there. Doing life together means that we don't always have a set curriculum that we use, but we are ready to face all that life dishes out to and through our kids. We reinforce good choices when we see our children exercise wisdom. And we use their failures to teach them about God's grace, to guide them instead of ignoring them or shaming them.

We would never claim to be perfect fathers. (Our kids wouldn't give us the title either!) We make mistakes, and our children make mistakes. We discipline our children, but we also seek to recast their mistakes and flaws into learning opportunities. We've seen parents who, having extremely high expectations for obedience and compliance from their children, unravel when their child makes a bad choice. We've also seen parents who are rarely involved in their child's life, and their son or daughter is left to figure out life on their own. Neither of these approaches is good. There is a healthier, biblically balanced approach. We know that failures are inevitable, so we shouldn't be surprised when our children disobey or lie or fail to meet our expectations. It seems inconceivable when you first hold your infant that your child will make wrong choices or could someday be overcome by evil. But that's the reality of life in our fallen world. The real question is not "if" it happens, but "when." What will you say to a son or daughter when that happens? We need to parent in a way that understands failure in light of the gospel, in light of God's grace.

To teach and parent in the context of real life means you must be prepared. You'll need to think about potential challenges. You'll need to be ready to say, "I don't know, but let me think about it and we can talk." You'll need to talk with other parents who have gone through similar struggles and to learn from those experiences. This isn't easy! Have you thought about how you will guide your kids when they encounter pornography? How will you counsel them about the difference between appearance and character? A teaching opportunity will arise when you least expect it. It can happen with a late-night phone call that delivers trouble or with an attitude that crops up unexpectedly and festers into decay. This is the God-given call of responsible parenting. The information you share with your children will often be best received when it comes in the context of relationships and experiences.

Relationships + Experiences + Information (+ Practices)

Earlier, we mentioned that these three components—relationships, extraordinary experiences, and information—form the acronym REI. There is one final component we want to add. Something else is needed to make sure that our REI truly leads to an adventure with God for our children. It's practices. There are spiritual practices that enable our kids to absorb all that we've been talking about.

Greg loves to climb mountains. Big mountains. And the first question people ask him about climbing is why he likes it so much. He says that while some people like to look at pictures, he likes to live them. Watching the sunrise from a mountaintop is absolutely breathtaking.

The second question people ask about climbing is how to train. The answer is embarrassingly simple: Do push-ups and sit-ups every day—and walk. Walk up and down hills carrying a thirty-pound pack. Walk up and down, up and down, up and down. Walk until your cardio is ready to carry you up a mountain.

If we want our children to experience a life of adventure as they follow Jesus, they need to practice. What does it mean to practice? Our children will tell you that we spent time every week memorizing Bible verses with them, reading the Bible on a daily basis, praying together every night, attending church regularly, and teaching them to give of their small financial resources. These are not as adventurous or disruptive as missions trips and retreats, but they are necessary practices that children need to become kingdom bringers. We know people who spend a great deal of time planning their children's educational development, career path, sports career, and artistic advancement. But very few actually put a strategic plan in place for their child's spiritual development. Yet spiritual practices undergird and support the relationships, experiences, and information you provide. They are part of the ordinary day-to-day role of parenting and raising your child to love and follow Jesus.

When Greg's daughter, Tabitha, entered her freshman year of high school, Greg and his wife spent a lot of time preparing a spiritual development plan for Tabitha's last four years at home (expecting her to leave for college after that). Imagine that your own son or daughter is leaving home in just four years. What would you do to prepare your child spiritually to step out alone into the world? Greg and Julie put together a plan where Tabitha would read books with them, such as *The Case for Christ* and *The Case for Faith* by Lee Strobel.[4] They'd read through the entire Bible together. They planned out two international missions trips to experience together. They looked at going through Dave Ramsey's Financial Peace University together. And, God willing, if enough money was saved, they would take her on a spiritual pilgrimage to Israel so she could follow in the footsteps of Jesus with them.

Leanne and Jimmy talked about a spiritual plan for their children, something they were committed to do on a regular daily or weekly basis. They memorized Scripture together, prayed individually with each child before bed each night, and worked hard to ensure that they never missed their family small group experience every Saturday night. They taught their children Bible verses that started with each letter of the alphabet so the Scriptures would be embedded in their minds as they learned their ABCs. (We've included this list of verses in the appendix, in case you want to do the same with your children.) And the Mellado family nightly prayer time became an amazing ritual where Mom and Dad went to each child's room, starting with the youngest. The agenda was simple: talk about the day, talk about whatever was on their kids' minds, go over the memory verses from time to time, and just let each child be the center of attention for ten to twenty well-spent minutes. Through simple family activities like these, children can increasingly learn to become kingdom bringers. Helping them to develop spiritual practices is part of the plan.

Ready to get started? Take a moment to think about the children in your life. Is there a relationship you've been neglecting? Are there experiences you want to give your kids? Sketch out some plans and ideas. Is there information you need to communicate to them? What are some simple practices you can implement? Don't worry about figuring it all out at once. Most parenting happens in the day-to-day small and seemingly inconsequential moments. But don't neglect these times. This is where life change happens.

CHAPTER 9

Caring for Children in Your Church

Church has believed that parents probably won't assume responsibility for their own children's growth, so they have tried to become a parent substitute. This in turn has fostered parents to adopt a "drop-off" mentality. Maybe the greatest gift a church can give parents is the confidence and courage to do what God has wired them to do.

—Reggie Joiner

The greatest influence a church may have in affecting children is by impacting their parents.

—George Barna

Greg grew up directly across the street from the church his family attended. Not only did they go to Sunday school and the morning worship service every weekend, they often went on Sunday night. Wednesday night youth group was rarely missed. The Wednesday night program started with Whirlybirds for the younger grades (where kids memorized Bible verses and had an emblem sewn on their beanies as a reward) and progressed into a vibrant gathering for high school students.

Mrs. Leib was the first-grade Sunday school teacher. Her energetic use of flannel-graph characters made the stories of the Bible come to life. Mr. Otto patiently taught the Gospels about Jesus to sixth-grade boys, who ruthlessly laughed at the hair growing out of Mr. Otto's ears. Norman Maynard was the longtime preacher, and children would fidget beside their parents through his sermons, because in those days they were all expected to attend "big church" with their moms and dads.

Not so today.

Children and Church Attendance

In his book *The American Church in Crisis*, David Olson reveals that 77 percent of Americans do not have a consistent, life-giving connection with a local church.[1] He further states that of the 23 percent who are considered "regular participants" in the life of a church, attendance has dropped dramatically—a regular participant is defined as a person who attends church at least three out of every eight Sundays.[2] In Greg's experience leading a megachurch and working with children's ministry leaders, they discovered that many children participated only one out of three weekends.

This isn't just a problem with the American church. Regular church attendance in the United Kingdom stands at 6 percent of the population, with the average age of attendees being fifty-one. This is a decline in church attendance since 1980, when regular attendance stood at 11 percent with an average age of thirty-seven. It is predicted that by 2020, attendance will be around 4 percent, with an average age of fifty-six.[3] Even though Australia has more churches (13,000) than schools (9,500), and the latest census shows that Christianity is the religion with which most Australians identify (61.1 percent), less than one in seven Australians who ticked "Christianity" on their census form regularly attend a church.[4]

This drop in church attendance creates dramatic challenges for churches that adhere to a traditional children's discipleship model, with children's classes during the weekend service as the primary mode of teaching children to follow Jesus.

So what is the alternative? How can we best care for children in our church? We believe there are four fundamental shifts that must take place among church leaders and the way they approach ministry to children.

1. First, the church must shift from a "we can disciple your kids and you can help" attitude to "you can disciple your kids and we can help."

2. Second, the church must shift from children's ministry as a support ministry that provides child care while adults attend the worship service to children's ministry that has a clear discipleship focus on training children to follow Jesus.

3. Third, the church must shift from age-segregated to age-integrated.

4. Fourth, the church must shift from children "receiving" to children "giving."

Shift 1: From "we can disciple your kids and you can help" to "you can disciple your kids and we can help." We were never intended to hire professionals to teach our children about Jesus. Or to allow professionals to show our children how to follow Jesus. Or to transfer the responsibility of discipling our children to others. As parents, grandparents, guardians, or caregivers, we are responsible for passing on our faith to the children God has entrusted into our care. As we discussed in the previous chapter, we are not meant to disciple our children alone. In fact, the commandments given in Deuteronomy 6 to pass our faith to our children were meant to be understood and lived out as a community of God followers, not just as individual households. However, the *primary* responsibility for the discipleship of children does not fall on the church community, but on the family unit.

With the rise of the Sunday school movement in the early twentieth century, the church began to take on additional responsibility for the discipleship of children. Previously, children attended church services with their parents, and the primary instruction of children was done in the home by the parents. Rather than equipping parents and caregivers to be the primary disciple makers, the church took on that role. In the church-centered model, church ministries assumed more and more responsibility for discipling children. Parents attended services with other adults and without their children.

Here is why this model doesn't work.

Let's assume that a child walks onto a stage pushing a toy shopping cart filled with forty multicolor plastic balls. Each ball represents one hour of time that the church has to impact the life of a child during one year. As a result of vacations, sports, illness, and so on, kids who regularly attend Sunday school do so about forty times a year. For many children, this is the only time that they hear about Jesus. Most children's ministries know this and are very intentional about what they're teaching so kids will hear about Jesus.

Why should the church be the only one to carry this responsibility? Why is this considered the norm? Back to our illustration. The child is back onstage pushing full-size shopping carts onto the stage. Each cart is filled with balls. Each ball represents one hour in a year that parents have an opportunity to influence their children. There are about three thousand balls in those carts, three thousand hours each year that parents have with their children. Those carts full of balls just keep on coming!

Three thousand versus forty. This visible discrepancy is a reminder to all who love and care for children in our church that as important as Sunday school and youth group and children's ministries are for children, they can never replace the impact of parents. That's not to say that churches are wasting their time. Our illustration is meant to demonstrate why a church's primary responsibility needs to be partnering with parents. Churches cannot just care for children an hour each week and hope that discipleship is happening in the home. Churches need to encourage parents. To empower parents.

What if every church developed an integrated approach to assist parents in discipling their children from birth through high school graduation? Church would no longer be something you did on weekends, but an experience that continued throughout the week. Discipleship would take place not only on Sunday but also in the home.

When you make the shift to "you (the parents) can disciple your children and we (the church) can help," you will experience opposition. There is a consumer mindset among many people attending church today, and when you begin to talk and teach about the need for them to engage in discipleship, some may feel you are passing the buck or they are not getting their "money's worth." Some have said to us, "The entire point of us bringing our kids to church is so that you can teach them." Others have pointed to the building and the investment they've made: "We helped pay for and build this beautiful children's area. Now it's time for us to see the return on our investment." Rather than getting defensive, a church leader's best response is to accept responsibility for the attitudes we have helped to develop. Patience is needed. Instruction is needed. Equipping must take place before people are ready to change to a new paradigm.

As we equip parents, we need to encourage them to rethink their "drop-off" mentality—"dropping off" the kids so the adults can be fed in "big church." The drop-off approach tends to reduce children's discipleship to a glorified nursery program, a holding space for supervising kids while the real work is done in the worship service. A purposeful children's discipleship program will inform and equip parents and give them opportunities to lead their children spiritually both at church and at home. We provide parents with safe opportunities to learn and practice the discipling of their children so they can do it in their own homes. If you are considering making this shift or are in the midst of such a shift, we want to encourage you to push through. The strategy of "we (the church) can disciple your children and you (the parents) can help" is not a biblical model. When you shift to the alternative, you will find yourself much more effective in impacting both children and parents.

Shift 2: From children's ministry as a support ministry to children's ministry as a central focus. To really disciple children and help them to follow Jesus, children's ministry in our churches must shift from being a support program to a ministry that is central to the mission of the church. The focus must be on discipling children as an end in itself—a worthy goal—and not as a means to attract and retain adults.

At the start of each of our weekend services at RiverTree, I (Greg) used to walk through our children's ministry halls. I'll admit, I wasn't there looking for a child to bless. I wasn't there to take some time to encourage a parent. I was making sure that our children's classes were fully staffed. That the atmosphere was warm and inviting. That none of the classes were closed because they were filled to capacity.

My checking on those things was not bad or wrong. Having

a fully staffed children's ministry that is warm and inviting and has room for visitors is a good thing. The problem wasn't with our ministry. It was my motivation. It was all wrong. I wasn't checking up to make sure that our children could be discipled effectively. I wanted to make sure that the parents were having a good experience so they would come back to church. I wanted to make sure that none of our classes were at or above 80 percent capacity, a size when people tend to feel crowded and leave. For me, children's ministry existed to support whatever we were doing in our weekend services. If I wanted to boost our weekend attendance, I would work with our children's director to have little kids do a "special song" during the services. I knew that more parents would come to hear their children sing. For me, children were a means to an end. The goal was church growth.

When I was planting my first church in Dublin, Ireland, our team discovered a very effective outreach event. We called it "Mom's Day Out." We would pass out flyers in a neighborhood explaining that every Monday afternoon from 2 to 4 p.m., we would provide games and a snack in a local park for children ages five to fourteen. At first the neighborhood moms were skeptical, hesitant to let strangers interact with their kids. But after a few weeks of sitting in the park watching us as we played with their little ones, they began to trust us and enjoyed their afternoon off.

There was nothing wrong with what we were doing, playing with kids and providing a snack. We would even throw in a creatively told Bible story. The problem, again, was my motivation. I wasn't leading our team in this ministry to bless and disciple the children. I was playing with the kids so that I could develop relationships with their parents and eventually build a new church.

Children were a means to an end. And for many years, this was how I operated. Until God opened my eyes. Until I saw the reality of the 4–14 window. Until I saw the unique opportunity we have to reach children with the good news of Jesus and to work with parents to disciple their children to be followers of Jesus. Knowing that 85 percent of those who choose to follow Jesus do so between the ages of four and fourteen, we should have people lined up to serve in children's ministry. But this won't happen unless children are highly valued within the church.

Think about your church budget. Does it reflect the value you place on children? Do you have representatives from your children's ministry involved in major church leadership decisions? If you are a pastor or senior church leader, are you personally involved in pouring into the lives of the children in the church you serve? Are children integrated into everything you do as a church? Until you can answer yes to these questions, you have not made the shift from children's ministry as a support service to children's ministry as central to the mission of your church.

Shift 3: From age-segregated to age-integrated. Finish this sentence: Children are to be seen and . . . Some of us grew up in a time when the natural response was that children are to be seen and *not heard.* Unfortunately, this old adage is still the norm in many churches. This attitude about children has been around for a long time. There is an incident in Matthew's gospel where a group of parents bring their children to Jesus so that he can pray for them and bless them. Jesus' disciples shooed the little kids away—respectable rabbis never paid attention to little ones. But Jesus rebuked his disciples: "Let the children alone, don't prevent them from coming to me. God's kingdom is made up of people like these" (Matt. 19:14 MSG).

Don't misunderstand. There are times when age-appropriate teaching needs to take place. We are not advocating that children should be integrated into every ministry in your church. It is appropriate and necessary for adults to have ministries that focus on their struggles, needs, and joys. Instead, we are challenging you to look for appropriate opportunities that would allow children to fully participate in the life of the church. We have attended church prayer services that were kid friendly. They included highly creative ways for adults and little ones to pray together. Multiple prayer stations were set up around the room so that adults and children could move from station to station to experience intimacy with God in a variety of multisensory ways. Some of the most profound and meaningful prayers we have heard have come from our children. And by the way, the adults love it!

At one prayer gathering, one station was run entirely by fourth graders. The children invited adults to join them in praying for their schools. In another instance, children's ministry leaders were brought onto the platform. Fourth- to eighth-grade students gathered around the leaders and prayed for them. It was profound to see the kids spiritually bless the adults! Kids don't have a miniature-size Holy Spirit! They have the Holy Spirit!

We don't believe that every weekend service the church offers should be fully age integrated. There are times when age-appropriate teaching is necessary. However, occasional age-integrated services can be incredibly effective and life giving for the entire church. Why not plan a teaching of the Passover (Seder) meal in which adults and children of all ages participate? Or how about during the weekend teaching, interview students about the struggles they face in school? This would be a tremendous opportunity to teach adults how to disciple children through those struggles.

It can also be incredibly healthy for families to worship together. For children to see their parents engaged in honoring God is a powerful modeling experience. Greg made a decision long ago to pray with his daughter, Tabitha, whenever an opportunity arose. While driving her to school one morning when she was fourteen, he asked her, "So what do you have going on today? How can I pray for you?" She told him about several tests, friendship challenges, and things she was looking forward to. So Greg said, "Okay, let's pray together." And he prayed for her. (No, no eyes were closed while driving.) At the end of the prayer, Tabitha asked, "How can I pray for you today, Dad?" And she prayed for her father, who was blown away.

Another time, Greg was saying bedtime prayers with Elijah, who was then six years old. As he was praying, Greg said he'd be flying to Colorado early the next morning. He asked Elijah if he would pray for safe travel. The point was really for Elijah to know why Daddy wouldn't be home when he woke up the next day. But Elijah immediately began to pray, "Dear God, please help my daddy be safe when he flies to Colorado." Never underestimate how much children can participate in the prayers of God's people.

At Greg's church, children are a regular part of the weekend services. Boys and girls ages five to ten are brought into the worship time of singing at the beginning of every service. When singing is done, the children return to their classes, where they receive age-appropriate Bible teaching. Families are frequently brought up on the main platform to recite Bible memory verses or to be interviewed about a way they are serving together. This is not a gimmick. It's a way to show that we value children. It also promotes parents as the primary disciplers of their little ones.

When special offerings are taken—to plant a new church, to help the homeless, to fill baby bottles with change for the crisis pregnancy center—children are encouraged to participate right along with adults. We've seen children empty their piggy banks to help those in need. And kids are encouraged to *earn* the money they give, not to simply give what their parents have given to them.

To be a church that truly cares for children, we must shift our emphasis to equipping parents and caregivers to disciple the ones God has entrusted to them. Children must be a central part of everything we do as a church. Integrating children into prayers, service opportunities, and giving initiatives shows who we are as a church.

Shift 4: From children receiving to children giving. Children aren't the church of tomorrow. Children are the church of today. Children have gifts and insights that are needed in the body of Christ. Yes, they need teaching and training, and they need to be discipled. Learning to be a disciple takes more than just passively listening to others. It involves responding and doing. We learn by listening *and* acting.

In healthy churches, we now regularly see high school students mentoring middle school students and middle school students mentoring those in the fourth and fifth grades.

One young teen we know started her own tennis shoe business to raise money for those in need. She would buy nondescript white shoes and artistically decorate them. The designer shoes became a hot item, and she had no shortage of customers. The local media picked up on her enterprise, and she was able to raise a good deal of money. She gave 100 percent of the profits to charity.

In the developing world, it is common to see students who are growing up in a Compassion child development center serving their local churches. These young people play in the band, are worship leaders, teach in children's classes, and are involved in a host of other serving opportunities. Having received, they share a common attitude of service to others. This is the opposite of some children who receive handouts from their parents without ever being asked to sacrifice and help others. In fact, one of the greatest dangers that children in the developed world face as they grow into their adolescent years is a sense of entitlement. The antidote to this entitlement mentality is being generous with their time, talents, and finances, and learning to give not just out of their abundance but in a way that could be considered a sacrifice. Unless we afford children the opportunity to be involved, to give back, to actively participate in the life of the church and community, we will reap what we sow—a generation that expects to receive rather than to give and invest in the lives of others.

The local church is God's chosen instrument of change for the world. Transforming the lives of children is the single most effective way to transform the life of the church. Children are not the church of tomorrow; they are the church of today.

CHAPTER 10

Caring for Children in Your Community

When I was very young, most of my childhood heroes wore capes, flew through the air, or picked up buildings with one arm. They were spectacular and got a lot of attention. But as I grew, my heroes changed, so that now I can honestly say that anyone who does anything to help a child is a hero to me.

—Mister Rogers

Every child you encounter is a divine appointment.

—Wess Stafford

A helpful tool that Greg developed to help people on their journey with Jesus in caring for children is something called Napkin Discipleship. Napkin Discipleship is a series of drawings that anyone can sketch on a napkin at their local Starbucks or McDonald's, or even in their own home. Simple is good!

One of the Napkin Discipleship tools that has been most helpful in teaching people to care for children in their community is called One Of.[1] When the drawing is completed, it looks like this:

FOR   WITH   ONE OF   IN

As we draw these figures, one at a time, we explain: God is *for* people. "For God loved the world so much that he gave his one and only Son, so that everyone who believes in him will not perish but have eternal life. God sent his Son into the world not to judge the world, but to save the world through him" (John 3:16–17). We want children to under-

stand that God sent Jesus not to judge the world, but to save the world. God is *for* people! And that is the good news!

Sadly, most people don't realize this. They feel far from God. But God didn't stop there. God isn't only *for* us; he is also *with* us.

We see this truth beginning in the Old Testament. God is *with* the nation of Israel as a cloud by day and a pillar of fire by night. God is *with* Moses as he speaks to him from a burning bush. God is *with* Joshua as Israel prepares to conquer the land. God is *with* Daniel in the lions' den. God is *with* Elijah on the mountain. The list goes on!

God's being *with* us is even better than God's being *for* us. But there is a problem when God is with us. God is very differ-ent from us. We are sinful, marred by our disobedience and selfishness. God is holy, and his otherness feels like an unbridgeable barrier. Most people feel sad and even afraid in his presence. The sad face with the baseball cap represents you and me! God's being *for* people and even being *with* people doesn't solve the problem.

Thankfully, God doesn't stop there. There's even better news: In Jesus, God becomes *one of* us. "For in Christ lives all the full-ness of God in a human body" (Col. 2:9). Eugene Peterson says it this way in *The Message*: "The Word became flesh and blood, and moved into the neighborhood" (John 1:14). God moved into the neighborhood and lived as one of us! Jesus lived as *one of* us, loves as *one of* us, even *likes us* while he is *one of* us.

God, in Jesus, puts on the baseball cap. As good as it is to know that God is *for* us and *with* us, it amazes us that God is *one of* us—and that he *likes* us! When most people discover this truth, they are no longer sad. *One of* is the crucial transition.

ONE OF

Now here's the best part:

When we understand the implications of God's being *for*, *with*, and *one of* us, that often compels us to invite Jesus to be *in* us. And that changes everything. God himself passes the DNA of Jesus into our very lives through the Holy Spirit, who empowers us to live as Jesus here on this earth.

IN

God's being *for*, *with*, and *one of* us pales in comparison to God's being *in* us. We are now walking around as "little Jesuses," filled with God's Spirit. We are God's kingdom bringers right here on earth.

So how does this change our lives? This means that, like God, we must be *for* people, *with* people, and *one of* the people we love and serve, so that the DNA of Jesus can be passed through our lives into the lives of others, and Jesus will then live *in* them as well.

For, With, One Of, In—and Caring for Children in Your Community

Many children today do not know that God is *for* them. They may even be inclined to believe that God is against them. A child living in extreme poverty might wonder if God is for him. A child whose

157

parents are divorcing could have similar doubts. A child on the outside of friendship circles at school probably would have some questions for God.

FOR

To really care for children in our community, we must do our best to communicate to every child we come in contact with that God is *for* every child. We have heard Wess Stafford assert over and over again, "In the heart of a child, one moment can last forever." It should be obvious to anyone that we, as followers of Jesus, are for children.

We are *for* children in the kind and encouraging words we speak. We are *for* children in the tender and appropriate touches we share. We are *for* children with the smiles we give. We are *for* children in the attention we offer.

Who are these children? They are the children we have regular contact with in our neighborhood and our networks of friends. They are the children we coach in sports leagues. They are the children our own kids play with after school. They are the children we spend time with at family gatherings.

They are also children we may encounter anywhere. It is the child who is kicking the back of our seat on a flight. It is the child waiting in line to sit on Santa's lap. It is the child sitting alone in the lunchroom when we are helping to serve. It is the child begging his mom for candy in the grocery store.

To care for children in our community, we must figure out

how we can bless every child we encounter. We must determine how we can show God's love for every child. In a world where so much seems to be against children, we must do our best to communicate that God is for them.

But being *for* children is not enough. As we see in our "One Of" Napkin Discipleship sketch, we must move to be *with* children.

Greg and Julie had to have some excavation done in the front yard of their home. A huge excavator sat right outside on their lawn. Their general contractor was a close friend and a committed follower of Jesus. He also loves children. Many of the subcontractors he employs reflect his heart for kids as well.

Greg and Julie's seven-year-old son, Elijah, was enamored with the work going on and especially with the "mighty machine" in their yard. At one point, the operator of the excavator stopped digging and knocked on Greg and Julie's front door. He asked Greg if it would be okay if Elijah rode in the excavator with him. He wanted to teach Elijah how to operate the piece of heavy equipment. Elijah was over the moon with excitement!

For the next thirty minutes, Elijah sat on the lap of the excavator operator and learned to dig with the big shovel. The man was really *with* Elijah. They were having fun together. And Elijah will never forget it.

Did the operator of the excavator have to take time out of his busy schedule to care for a child? Absolutely not. But this particular guy wants kids to know that he cares about them, and he shows them how much he cares by taking time to be *with* them.

With-Me Moments (Jimmy)

Think back to when you were a child. You probably had some adults in your life who took time to be with you. I had a coach whose willingness to be *with* me shaped my life. Coach Oliver coached my high school track team in Panama. During my freshman and sophomore years, this balding coach in his late forties did more than teach me techniques. He went way above and beyond what was expected. He invested in me. He cared about my life, about my character, about the choices I was making. To this day I remember three of the most powerful investments he made.

Coach Oliver looked beyond what benefited his track team and career. He cared about the future of his athletes. He saw an all-around ability in me for track and field beyond a single event. He saw potential that I did not see in myself. He envisioned me as a decathlete, competing in ten events. But the decathlon is not a high school event. What's more, the javelin was specifically forbidden. Teenage athletes and an eight-and-a-half-foot spear just don't mix! That made no difference to Coach Oliver. Since the school didn't even own a javelin, he purchased one with his own money. He expanded his coaching schedule to teach me the basics of throwing the javelin and to train me for competitions beyond high school. None of it ever helped the team. It never won us a single meet. It was simply his recognition of potential he wanted to foster for a day yet to come.

He developed my character as well. As my ability in the high jump outpaced that of my team and competitors, I developed a bit of an attitude. I would routinely set the bar 8 to 10 inches above the previous competitor's setting. When I cleared it, all was well with the world. During one meet, however, I missed. I came out of the pit angry and stomped around in disgust. *How could I miss that? I'm way better than this.*

Coach Oliver was right there, in my face. He took me aside and laid into me in the best way possible. He didn't yell or make a public display, but he let me know in no uncertain terms that my public tantrum offended him and my teammates. My tantrum sent a message to everyone that I felt superior to them. "Think about it. How does that make them feel?" he asked. "Does that tell them they must be really bad if they can't compete at your level?"

The message was clear. It's great to pursue excellence, but never let your pursuit denigrate or insult those around you.

And Coach Oliver taught me how to win with humility. I had never learned how to accept congratulations in a gracious way. A response like "I could have done better" wasn't needed. My false humility was wrong too. "Jimmy, all you have to say is, 'Thank you. I appreciate that,'" Coach Oliver said. "Nothing more than that is needed."

Did Coach Oliver's with-me moments change the trajectory of my life? Not really. I would have been an athlete with or without his influence. But his being with me for my benefit alone, with no benefit to himself or the team, changed my character.

Being *with* Children

How can we be *with* children? We engage them in meaningful conversation. We ask prompting questions and listen to their replies. We show that we are listening and that we care. If Greg asks his daughter, Tabitha, how school went today, Tabitha's typical reply is "Fine." If he asks her if anything special happened at school,

Tabitha will usually share a story about an interaction with a friend at lunch or how a teacher aggravated her or even talk about a challenging relationship with a boy. The key is for Greg to ask the right question and to be genuinely interested in her response.

We can also be *with* children by including them in our projects. Greg's dad is an incredibly gifted handyman. He can build or fix anything around the house. Unfortunately, when he included Greg in his home projects, it was usually to be his gofer or cleanup boy. Greg admits that he is not nearly as skilled as his father when it comes to fixing things. We are *with* children when we pass on skills—cooking, making crafts, passing a football, memorizing Bible verses, serving our neighbors. We are with them when we help them learn things they might not otherwise have an opportunity to learn.

One of our favorite ways to be *with* children is to read with them. Story time is an amazing way to connect with kids. Reading a book and using a different voice for each character is engaging and fun. Reading simple Bible stories with children embeds God's Word in their heart. Reading books that express a parent's love, or a friend's love, gives us an opportunity to say, "And that's how God loves you," or, "And that's how I love you."

One of the best ways we can be *with* children is to invite them into our world. We both travel a great deal. Our own children and other children with whom we spend time love to hear about what we have been doing. Children want to know about our work and our struggles, our triumphs and foul-ups. Children learn from our experiences.

Being *One Of*

The next step can be a bit more challenging but is absolutely vital if we want to impact the lives of the children around us. We must do our best to become *one of* them.

ONE OF

Jesus said we must become like children (Matt. 18:3). To become *one of* the children in your life, you must in so many ways become childlike.

Several years ago, Wess Stafford came over to the Nettles' home for dinner. As Greg and his wife finished the final preparations for their meal, Greg noticed that Wess was missing. "Where's Wess?" he asked Julie.

"I have no idea," she said.

So Greg made his way upstairs to Tabitha's room. She was four at the time. He peeked into the room and saw Wess's rear end sticking out of the cubbyhole attic. He and Tabitha were laughing uproariously as she showed him her secret hideout.

Sometimes, as adults, we think we're too old to engage at a child's level. We may be preoccupied with our own concerns or embarrassed that we'll look foolish, or we may have even forgotten how to play and talk with a child. But if we want to love children as God loves them, we need to become like a child. We need to become one of the kids again.

Rich Mullins wrote a song titled "Boy Like Me, Man Like

You." In the song he asks Jesus some questions: "Did you wrestle with a dog and lick his nose? Did you play beneath the spray of a water hose? Did you ever make angels in the winter snow?" Rich is really asking, "Jesus, when you were a boy, did you have fun?" And the answer is of course Jesus had fun! He was a child just like each of us was a child—just like every child we encounter. If we want to be *one of* the children in our lives, then we have to recover the perspective of a child. We may need a refresher course in having fun.

Our friend Ben has made several trips to South America with us. Invariably, when we visit children, Ben is a child magnet. He does magic tricks for the kids. He pulls quarters out of their ears. He makes small objects disappear. He even makes handkerchiefs turn colors. The children love Ben because he is having fun with them. Their laughter breaks down barriers. Parents in any culture love it when we make their children giggle.

Children want to be with adults who are fun to be around. So make the baseball team you coach fun to be a part of. Throw snow at each other as you're shoveling your neighbor's drive with their nine-year-old. Smear icing on the four-year-old's nose as you're icing cookies together. Even as adults, we want to be around people who cause us to lighten up. We become childlike when we abandon the image we are trying to portray and simply laugh together. Kids don't worry about image—what they look like to others. Greg's son, Elijah, will run down a hallway at church and do a headfirst slide into an imaginary home plate. Pretty soon a small group of children will have joined him in his impromptu baseball game. Eventually several adults will be catching and throwing baseballs that no one can see. It's an eruption of fun.

Elijah's best friend is his Poppop (Grandpa). Elijah's face lights up whenever Poppop stops over for a visit. Despite being seventy-eight years old, Poppop will get down on the floor to play cars with Elijah. He becomes the mountain on which Elijah climbs. If there is lawn mowing to do, Elijah sits on Poppop's lap on the tractor as they go up and down the yard time and time again. Poppop knows what it means to become *one of* Elijah's friends.

I See You

Among the tribes of northern Natal in South Africa, the most common greeting, equivalent to "hello" in English, is the expression *sawu bona*. It literally means "I see you." If you are a member of the tribe, you would reply by saying, "*Sikhona*," or "I am here." The order of the exchange is important: Until you see me, I do not exist. It's as if when you see someone, you bring them into existence.

When Elijah was two years old, he would stand in front of Greg and clap his hands when Greg was watching television. Greg would say, "I see you, Elijah." But he would continue to clap and to watch his dad. He wanted to know if his father *really* saw him or if his attention had quickly returned to the TV. "Daddy, do you really know that I am here?" Sometimes Greg would mute the TV so he could place his full attention on Elijah or take him into his lap. He wanted Elijah to know that he was seen. That he really mattered.

Part of being a friend to a child—part of being *one of*—means that we really see children. They know when we see them, and they know when we are too busy to really engage with them. Friends see one another not just in a literal sense, but in a heartfelt, soul-connecting, affirming way.

Nobel Prize–winning novelist Toni Morrison was asked why she had become a great writer. Was it the books she had read? Her discipline in writing? She laughed and said, "Oh, no, that is not why I am a great writer. I am a great writer because when I was a little girl and walked into a room where my father was sitting, his eyes would light up. That is why I am a great writer. That is why. There isn't any other reason."[2]

For those of us who interact with children, Toni's response may come as a bit of a surprise, maybe as a bit of encouragement and a bit of a wake-up call. When a child walks into the room, do we have "bright eyes"? Kids can tell. They know if you are *one of* them or if you are consumed with your own agenda.

Spend Time Together

We often use the phrase "spending time together." Time is our most valuable commodity, and we all want to spend our time wisely. Unfortunately, with all of the demands on how we spend our time—work, church, chores, paying bills—children may receive very little of this precious treasure. But that's what it means to love someone. You invest time in one another. Have you ever watched children playing together? They can run around for two hours, and when you tell them it's time to go, they say, "But we just got here!" If we want to become *one of* the children we encounter, then time is a commodity that we must invest freely in them.

One of our favorite ways to invest in children is to have an open dinner table. Our children's friends are always welcome to eat with us in our home. Sharing a meal can be a great way to invest time in the lives of those we want to become *one of.* As we eat, we typically play a game called "High/Low." It involves two simple questions that everyone around the table must answer. "What was your high of the day?" and "What was your low of the day?" Everyone has to have a high, but not everyone has to have a low. If you don't have a low, then everyone at the table does a rhythmical chant about "no low, no low." This game is great fun and draws out meaningful conversation about what is going on in our lives.

Greg's wife, Julie, is a Big Sister to a teenage girl named Rose. When Julie got involved with the Big Brother/Big Sister program, they explained that the most important thing she could do was to spend time with her little sis. The Big Sister idea is simply to pair an adult with a child who could use some help in her life. Julie shares meals with Rose, regularly has her in her home, takes her shopping, and just hangs out with her. Julie has become a significant *one of* in Rose's life.

Which leads us to the final but very important step in caring for children in our community.

Being *for* children, being *with* children, and becoming *one of* the children offers us the opportunity to speak God's truth into their lives. It allows the DNA of Jesus to be passed from our life into their life. Invariably, when we reach the point of becoming *one of* the children in our community, situations occur that give us an opportunity not only to live God's truth but also to verbalize God's truth. To tell a child that God's deepest desire is to have a meaningful relationship with them. To assure a child that God has a wondrous plan for their life. To walk a child through the process of inviting Jesus to be both their Savior and Lord. For children to experience what it means to have Jesus live *in us.*

When it comes to caring for children in our community, living out *for*, *with*, *one of*, and *in* is essential. With 85 percent of those who become followers of Jesus doing so between the ages of four and fourteen, being *for* children, *with* children, and *one of* the children is a way for us to pass our faith on to children so they can invite Jesus to live *in* their lives.

CHAPTER 11

Until Every Child Has a Church

Consider the facts. People are much more likely to accept Christ as their Savior when they are young.

—George Barna

Speak up for those who cannot speak for themselves, for the rights of all who are destitute.

—Proverbs 31:8 NIV

In this book, we've laid out a vision for seeing that small matters. Children matter to God. "Jesus said, 'Let the little children come to me, and do not hinder them, for the kingdom of heaven belongs to such as these'" (Matt. 19:14 NIV). Our hope is that your heart is alive to God's vision for loving and reaching children in your home, your community, your local church, and around the world.

Kids Love Church

One little girl in Ohio came up with her own plan. Kevin Rush and his family planted City Edge Church in Cleveland. One Saturday, Kevin was working on his sermon in his home office. He decided to take a coffee break. He walked into the next room and watched as his six-year-old daughter, Selah, was placing chairs in straight rows. He asked, "Hey, Selah, what are you doing?"

And Selah replied, "I'm starting a church."

Kevin prodded a bit. "What's your church about?"

"My church is called KidsLoveChurch.com. It's where kids love church."

"Really? Tell me what you do at KidsLoveChurch."

"At KidsLoveChurch.com, we love kids. We go to the park and throw parties. We serve people. We act out Bible stories. We clean up the park. We invite people to be part of us. We always have room for more friends to come join us."

"That sounds awesome! What are all these papers you cut out and put on each chair?"

"Daddy, that's money."

Kevin wondered what his daughter had picked up from him about money and the church. Was she going to be asking people for money? "Well, what's the money for?"

And Selah said, "The money is for us to give away to bless people and to start new churches."

How different life would be for Selah and her young friends if they didn't have the local church. We love it when children lead the way in making sure every child has a church because they have experienced what it means to have a church.

Church Planting

Parkview Church, led by our friend Tim Harlow, made the decision to plant a new church in Santa Elena, Ecuador. A group of us went to visit this fledgling church when it was two years old. The church was thriving and caring for more than 250 children through sponsorship ministries.

The highlight of the visit was when six of us visited one of the church families in their home. The house, though dirt-floored and tiny for the five-member family, was filled with laughter, singing, and an obvious love for God. The father is a breadmaker by trade. He also plays guitar and leads worship in his church. The three young children sang a worship song for us while Dad played guitar. Mom looked on with pride. This was obviously a very blessed family.

The amazing part of the story? Two years earlier, the church where this family would hear the good news of Jesus Christ did not exist. The mother and father of the three children were not married. The family unit was in jeopardy. That's when Parkview Church entered the picture, when Tim Harlow boldly stated that the church he leads would partner with Stadia and Compassion to plant a new church. Six months later, the new church opened, and the three children were registered in Compassion's child development program.

This bread-baking, singing family became part of this new body of Christ. First, the mom gave her life to Jesus, and shortly after, the dad accepted Jesus as his Savior. Today, the entire family centers their life around God's Word.

One of the first things the father did was go to his pastor and ask him to perform the marriage ceremony for him and the woman with whom he was living. Their three children now have committed parents. They are growing up in a secure environment where their dad's love for their mom models Christ's love for the church.

At the end of our visit with this family, they proudly served us fresh-baked bread. The father handed me (Greg) a small loaf, and I couldn't help but think of the words "This is the body of Christ, take and eat."

Where would this family be without this local church? Every child needs a church!

A Special Baptism Weekend (Greg)

I can still remember when Tabitha was eleven years old. We were having a baptism weekend at our church, and I preached a clear message on what it means to become a follower of Jesus. At the end of the message, I invited people to take the step of being baptized into Christ. More than a hundred people responded!

About halfway through this amazing baptism experience, I looked up at the steps of the baptistery and there was my daughter, Tabitha! She walked down into the water with me and confessed Jesus as her Savior and Lord of her life, and I had the unbelievable privilege of baptizing her. I am grateful for churches like ours that help families disciple their children. The goal is that one day all these children will make the decision to become followers of Jesus.

But what if there was no church? Where would children like Tabitha learn how much God loves them? This was the case for young Kizel in Bolivia. There was no church for her to attend. Hundreds of children living in Kizel's village had never had an opportunity to hear how much God loves them. That all changed when a new church was planted in her village.

For Kizel, the partnership between church and children's ministry has transformed her life. A new church was planted in her hometown, and at the age of six, Kizel was registered for Compassion International sponsorship and began attending programs at the new church. Kizel's sponsor was Tabitha. She was fourteen. Two years after Tabitha began this relationship, I visited Kizel at her church. I met with Compassion's project director. In her office, a wall was covered with binders, one for each child in the program. Each binder is a year-by-year history of a child's life. She pulled the binder for Kizel and showed me her school records. She is a very bright young girl—in fact, Kizel is the best in her school academically. What pleased me most was Kizel's church record. Kizel never misses Sunday school. I asked the project director about the red heart beside Kizel's name. She explained that in June of that year, Kizel had accepted Jesus as her Savior and asked him to be Lord of her life. My knees went weak.

Salvation is the work of God. Kizel came to know Jesus because she heard the gospel message and God worked in her heart, revealing his love for her. God used his church to bring that message to her. A church in the United States became others-focused and invested its resources to plant that church in Bolivia. A fourteen-year-old girl named Tabitha became others-focused and sponsored a little girl named Kizel in that new church. As a result, Kizel made the decision to follow Jesus that transforms her for all eternity. And in the process, Tabitha was transformed as well.

Making Joyful Noises (Jimmy)

I can't remember a time growing up when we weren't part of a church. Actually, we didn't use the phrase "going to church" because the church was fully integrated into our lives. Church was less a place we went to than a community where we belonged. My parents did everything they could to make sure we were involved.

This wasn't easy. Since we moved around a lot, we often lived in a hotel for several weeks while we looked for a home. It would have been easy for Mom and Dad to create "vacation Sundays" and bag the idea of church. They were far more sincere and creative. While we waited to find a place to live and a church to attend, Sunday morning became family church where family was the "staff." Each one of us had a role. My sister led the worship—we sang together. My brother tapped into the flannel graphs and supplies from my mother's children's ministry—we learned together. I was in charge of the offering—we gave together. My tiniest sister got to be the congregation!

There was an amazing wisdom in this approach. When we didn't have a local church to attend, we were still the church gathered together under the Mellado family name. Each of us participated. We didn't sit back and just watch. We were leading, serving, doing what we could do. Mom made sure we understood that we were there to serve. "Never let anyone look down on you because you are young, *niños*," she would tell us, citing Paul's admonition to Timothy in the New Testament. We understood. We worshiped. We served. We celebrated the Lord's Supper. Our parents discipled us through the experience.

Once we found our church, Mom and Dad—and the family they led—were all in. Even in the most dangerous neighborhood in Managua in Nicaragua, Mom took her four children by the hand and guided us through the streets to Wednesday evening Bible study. Dad might be on the road traveling, but so was Mom. She was on her way to church and always with her children.

Mom made sure to include us in worship with the adults in addition to Sunday school if it was offered. Worship was vibrant. Energetic. Full of life—and so marked by joy I can still experience it in my mind four decades later. Music in Latin America is central to life, and church music is no exception. There were mornings when the rain pelted down so hard on the corrugated metal roof that we couldn't hear the pastor speak. But the downpours couldn't muffle the singing, the clapping, and the music of our simple congregation as it fully leaned into worship.

When I visit Compassion program churches and the Compassion-Stadia churches we are planting today, I experience the same passionate worship—with children front and center. I am amazed at the prominent roles children play in these churches in Latin America. Little girls interpret the music and give praise through dance, song after song. Musicians in their teens play a vital role in praise bands. Children share the Scripture. None of these are occasional programs or special performances. They are woven into the life of worship Sunday after Sunday. Children count in church worship. Family worship counts in the kingdom of heaven.

Now that I'm the head of Compassion International, nothing gives me more pleasure than to see local churches meeting real needs of the children in their congregations and giving children a place to serve. I believe a portion of my passion was shaped years ago in the hotels, living rooms, and sanctuaries where we worshiped as a family. From dirt floors to concrete slabs to sanctuaries swathed in plush carpet, biblically functioning churches shaped me to care for children yet to be shaped today.

The authors in Bolivia

Two Billion Children

The apostle Paul writes, "But how can they call on [Jesus] to save them unless they believe in him? And how can they believe in him if they have never heard about him? And how can they hear about him unless someone tells them?" (Rom. 10:14).

Today there are more than seven billion people on planet Earth. Nearly two billion of the world's population are children under the age of eighteen.[1] Millions upon millions of these children do not have access to a local church. Planting new churches remains the single most effective way to reach people with the good news of Jesus Christ. A full 85 percent of those who choose to follow Jesus do so between the ages of four and fourteen, that 4–14 window. Planting new churches that create a plan to care for children produces exponential kingdom results. Every child must have a church.

Every twenty-four hours, 21,000 children die of poverty or poverty-related preventable diseases. That's 147,000 children every week. More than 7.5 million every year.[2] These are staggering numbers. It's hard to grasp the magnitude of such devastation. Such loss.

One way that Greg illustrates the number of children who die every day is with steel BBs. He places 21,000 BBs in two clear plastic water pitchers. He sets a tin trough on two wooden stools. Beneath the tin trough he places a microphone to amplify the sound. As he explains to his audience the number of children who die every day, he slowly pours the BBs into the tin trough. The sound is deafening throughout the room—and in the hearts of those hearing it. He keeps pouring, and the sound simply becomes static, never-ending. It is hard to imagine that this kind of loss of life takes place day after day, week after week, year after year.

At the end of his demonstration, Greg removes one BB. This BB represents the life of a child you can help. He encourages those in attendance to step forward and take a BB from the trough if they are willing to sponsor a child. Without exception, the line is long with people coming forward to pick out a BB—people ready to sponsor a child. It is a beautiful sight.

Every child is at risk. Dangers and diseases stem from both poverty and prosperity. But the gospel overcomes these risks.

We want parents, pastors, children's ministry directors, volunteers, coaches, teachers, and anyone else who cares about children to tell others that children matter—to raise the bar in discipling, to raise up children to follow Jesus. But it takes a church—a community of committed Jesus followers—to make all this happen.

We won't stop until every child has a church!

We won't stop praying until every child has a church!

We won't stop investing until every child has a church!

We won't stop proclaiming how much God values children until every child has a church!

We won't stop caring for the children in our homes until every child has a church!

We won't stop caring for the children in our community until every child has a church!

We won't stop caring for children in our churches until every child has a church!

We won't stop planting new churches until every child has a church!

We won't stop sponsoring children until every child has a church!

With the message and the presence of Jesus, we can release children from the dangers and diseases of poverty and prosperity. We as parents, caregivers, neighbors, churches, and new church planters can raise up a generation of world-changing children.

Will you join us? We can give you one good reason why you should.

Small matters!

ABC Bible Verses

Verse	Version	Scripture
Rom. 8:28	NIV	**A**nd we know that in all things God works for the good of those who love him, who have been called according to his purpose.
Acts 16:31	NIV	**B**elieve in the Lord Jesus, and you will be saved—you and your household.
Eph. 6:1	NIV	**C**hildren, obey your parents in the Lord, for this is right.
James 4:8	KJV	**D**raw nigh to God, and he will draw nigh to you.
Prov. 20:11	NIV	**E**ven small children are known by their actions, so is their conduct really pure and upright?
John 3:16	NIV	**F**or God so loved the world that he gave his one and only Son, that whoever believes in him shall not perish but have eternal life.
1 John 4:4b	KJV	**G**reater is he that is in you, than he that is in the world.
Isa. 6:8b	NIV	**H**ere am I. Send me!
Gen. 1:1	NIV	**I**n the beginning God created the heavens and the earth.

Matt. 7:1	KJV	**J**udge not, that ye be not judged.
Ps. 34:13	NIV	**K**eep your tongue from evil and your lips from telling lies.
Matt. 28:20b	KJV	**L**o, I am with you always, even unto the end of the world. Amen.
Prov. 23:26	NIV	**M**y son, give me your heart and let your eyes delight in my ways.
2 Cor. 6:2b	NIV	**N**ow is the day of salvation.
Ps. 106:1	KJV	**O** give thanks unto the LORD; for he is good: for his mercy endureth for ever.
James 5:16b	KJV	**P**ray one for another.
1 Thess. 5:19	KJV	**Q**uench not the Spirit.
Eccl. 12:1	KJV	**R**emember now thy Creator in the days of thy youth.
Matt. 7:14	KJV	**S**trait is the gate, and narrow is the way, which leadeth unto life.
1 Cor. 15:57	NIV	**T**hanks be to God! He gives us the victory through our Lord Jesus Christ.
Luke 2:11	KJV	**U**nto you is born this day, in the city of David a Saviour, which is Christ the Lord.
John 6:47	NIV	**V**ery truly I tell you, whoever believes has eternal life.
Ps. 51:7b	NIV	**W**ash me, and I will be whiter than snow.
Ps. 8:1	KJV	How e**X**cellent is thy name in all the earth! who hast set thy glory above the heavens.
Matt. 5:14	NIV	**Y**ou are the light of the world. A city on a hill cannot be hidden.
Luke 19:5–6	NIV	"**Z**acchaeus, come down immediately. I must stay at your house today." So he came down at once and welcomed him gladly.

Notes

Chapter 1: Children at Risk

1. Senate Committee on the Judiciary, "Children, Violence, and the Media: A Report for Parents and Policy Makers," September 14, 1999, accessed June 14, 2006. Previously available at *http://judiciary.senate.gov/oldsite/mediavio.htm*.

2. Amnesty International, "Child Soldiers: From Cradle to War," *http://www.amnestyusa.org/our-work/issues/children-s-rights/child-soldiers*.

3. UN News Centre, "Number of Children Affected by Conflict in Syria Has Doubled Since Last Year," March 10, 2014, *http://www.un.org/apps/news/story.asp?NewsID=47320#.Ve7iksY2ttc*.

4. Centers for Disease Control and Prevention, "Youth Risk Behavior Surveillance: United States, 2013," Morbidity and Mortality Weekly Report, *Surveillance Summaries* 63, no. 4 (June 13, 2014), *http://www.cdc.gov/mmwr/pdf/ss/ss6304.pdf?utm_source=rss&utm_medium=rss&utm_campaign=youth-risk-behavior-surveillance-united-states-2013-pdf*.

5. UNESCO, Institute for Statistics, "Children out of School: Measuring Exclusion from Primary Education," 2005, *http://www.uis.unesco.org/Library/Documents/oosc05-en.pdf*.

6. Eleanor Goldberg, "Sex Trafficking Isn't an 'Over There' Issue: 100,000 US Kids Are Sold into It Every Year," *Huffington Post*, Nov. 3, 2014, *http://www.huffingtonpost.com/2014/11/02/sex-trafficking-kids-us_n_6083890.html*.

7. Carol Ronken and Hetty Johnston, "Child Sexual Assault: Facts and Statistics," Australian Institute of Criminology, 1993, Bravehearts, December 2012, *https://www.bravehearts.org.au/files/Facts%20and%20Stats_updated141212.pdf*.

8. "Global Sex Trafficking Fact Sheet," Equality Now, *http://www .equalitynow.org/node/1010.*

9. World Bank Group, "Report Finds 400 Million Children Living in Extreme Poverty," October 10, 2013, The World Bank, *http://www.worldbank.org/en/news/press-release/2013/10/10/ report-finds-400-million-children-living-extreme-poverty.*

10. UNICEF, "Millennium Development Goals: 1. Eradicate Extreme Poverty and Hunger," *http://www.unicef.org/mdg/poverty.html.*

11. Ibid.

12. Ibid.

13. Commission on Ending Childhood Obesity, "Draft Final Report of the Commission on Ending Childhood Obesity," September 29, 2015, World Health Organization, *http://www.who.int/end-childhood-obesity/en/.*

14. Scott C. Todd, *Hope Rising: How Christians Can End Extreme Poverty in This Generation* (Nashville: Nelson, 2014).

15. Ibid., 22.

16. Ibid.

17. Ibid., 23.

18. Ibid.

19. Ibid., 24.

20. "Millennials in the Workplace: Executive Summary," Bentley University, *http://www.bentley.edu/centers/center-for-women-and -business/millennials-workplace.*

21. Leigh Buchanan, *Meet the Millennials*, quoted in Jay Gilbert, "The Millennials: A New Generation of Employees, a New Set of Engagement Policies," *Ivey Business Journal*, September/October 2011, *http://iveybusinessjournal.com/publication/the-millennials-a -new-generation-of-employees-a-new-set-of-engagement-policies/.*

22. Tom Petruno, "Beyond Profits: Millennials Embrace Investing for Social Good," *Los Angeles Times*, December 7, 2014, *http://www .latimes.com/business/la-fi-socially-conscious-investing-20141207-story .html#page=1.*

23. Bryant Myers, "The State of the World's Children: A Cultural

Challenge to the Christian Mission in the 1990s," presented at an Evangelical Foreign Mission Association executive retreat.

Chapter 2: Wrecked (Greg's Story)

1. Wess Stafford, *Too Small to Ignore: Why the Least of These Matters Most* (Colorado Springs: WaterBrook, 2007).

Chapter 5: What Love Does

1. The people of RiverTree gave $160,000, enough to plant two new churches in Colombia!

Chapter 6: Enough Is Enough

1. Amber Von Schooneveld, *Hope Lives: A Journey of Restoration* (Loveland, CO: Group, 2008), 109.
2. "Waste and Recycling: Recycling and Energy Recovery," previously available at PWC, *http://www.pwc.com/en_US/us/about-us/corporate-responsibility/corporate-responsibility-report/assets/pdf/1-pwc-sustainability-6–8-lesson.pdf*.
3. "World Population Data Sheet 2014," Population Reference Bureau, *http://www.prb.org/publications/datasheets/2014/2014-world-population-data-sheet.aspx*.
4. Bruce Wydick, "Does International Child Sponsorship Work? New Research Says Yes," *Journal of Political Economy*, April 2013. For a summary statement, see University of Chicago Press, *http://press.uchicago.edu/pressReleases/2013/April/0413JPEpr.html*.
5. Rob Kerby, "Church Kids Less Likely to Divorce or Live in Poverty," 2011, Beliefnet, *http://www.beliefnet.com/columnists/on_the_front_lines_of_the_culture_wars/2011/08/church-kids-are-less-likely-to-divorce-or-live-in-poverty.html#ixzz3dKKBEUwF*.
6. Global Alliance for Incinerator Alternatives, "Consumption: Our Current Consumption Habits Are Fueling a Global Environmental Crisis . . .," GAIA, *http://www.no-burn.org/section.php?id=89*.
7. Ibid.

Chapter 7: The Window

1. "World Population Data Sheet 2014," Population Reference Bureau, *http://www.prb.org/publications/datasheets/2014/2014-world -population-data-sheet.aspx.*

2. Anup Shah, "Poverty Facts and Stats," January 7, 2013, Global Issues, *http://www.globalissues.org/article/26/poverty-facts-and-stats.*

3. Bruce Wydick, "Does International Child Sponsorship Work? New Research Says Yes," *Jounal of Political Economy*, April 2013. For a summary statement, see University of Chicago Press, *http://press .uchicago.edu/pressReleases/2013/April/0413JPEpr.html.*

4. Rob Kerby, "Church Kids Less Likely to Divorce or Live in Poverty," Beliefnet, *http://www.beliefnet.com/columnists/on_the_ front_lines_of_the_culture_wars/2011/08/church-kids-are-less-likely -to-divorce-or-live-in-poverty.html#ixzz3dKKBEUwF.*

Chapter 8: Caring for Children in Your Home

1. Whenever I tell this story, people invariably ask, "So what are rules number one and two?" Rule 1: The most important thing I can do today is deepen my relationship with God. Rule 2: Treat Julie (my wife) more kindly than anyone else.

2. Bob Goff, *Love Does: Discover a Secretly Incredible Life in an Ordinary World* (Nashville: Nelson, 2012).

3. US Department of Agriculture's 2012 Annual Report "Expenditures on Children by Families."

4. Lee Strobel, *The Case for Christ: A Journalist's Personal Investigation of the Evidence for Jesus* (Grand Rapids, MI: Zondervan, 1998); Strobel, *The Case for Faith: A Journalist Investigates the Toughest Objections to Christianity* (Grand Rapids, MI: Zondervan, 2000).

Chapter 9: Caring for Children in Your Church

1. David T. Olson, *The American Church in Crisis: Groundbreaking Research Based on a Database of Over 200,000 Churches* (Grand Rapids, MI: Zondervan, 2008), 30.

2. Ibid., 29.

3. WhyChurch, *http://www.whychurch.org.uk/trends.php*.

4. McCrindle Research, "Church Attendance in Australia," 2013, *The McCrindle Blog, http://www.mccrindle.com.au/the-mccrindle-blog/ church_attendance_in_australia_infographic*.

Chapter 10: Caring for Children in Your Community

1. One Of was developed by Greg Nettle and Alex Absalom. You can read more about this tool in their ebook *One Of* at *https://www .exponential.org/resource-ebooks/one-of/*.

2. Donald Miller, *Searching for God Knows What* (Nashville: Nelson, 2010).

Chapter 11: Until Every Child Has a Church

1. Anup Shah, "Poverty Facts and Stats," January 7, 2013, Global Issues, *http://www.globalissues.org/article/26/poverty-facts-and-stats*.

2. Scott C. Todd, *Hope Rising: How Christians Can End Extreme Poverty in This Generation* (Nashville: Nelson, 2014), 23.

ABOUT THE EXPONENTIAL SERIES

The interest in church planting has grown significantly in recent years. The need for new churches has never been greater. At the same time, the number of models and approaches is expanding. To address the unique opportunities of churches in this landscape, Exponential Network, in partnership with Leadership Network and Zondervan, launched the Exponential Series in 2010.

Books in this series:

- Tell the reproducing church story.
- Celebrate the diversity of models and approaches God is using to reproduce healthy congregations.
- Highlight the innovative and pioneering practices of healthy reproducing churches.
- Equip, inspire, and challenge kingdom-minded leaders with the tools they need in their journey of becoming reproducing church leaders.

Exponential exists to attract, inspire, and equip kingdom-minded leaders to engage in a movement of high-impact, reproducing churches. We provide a national voice for this movement through the Exponential Conference, the Exponential Initiative, Exponential Venture, and the Exponential Series.

Leadership Network exists to accelerate the impact of 100X leaders. Believing that meaningful conversations and strategic connections can change the world, we seek to help leaders navigate the future by exploring new ideas and finding application for each unique context.

For more information about the Exponential Series, go to *http://www.exponential.org/exponentialseries*.

Exponential Series Complete Set

Essential Resources for Church Planters and Missional Leaders

The *Exponential Series Complete Set* includes all ten volumes from the Exponential Series of books. It contains:

- *Discipleshift* by Jim Putman, Bobby Harrington, and Robert Coleman
- *Exponential* by Dave Ferguson and Jon Ferguson
- *Barefoot Church* by Brandon Hatmaker
- *On the Verge* by Alan Hirsch and Dave Ferguson
- *Sifted* by Wayne Cordeiro with Francis Chan and Larry Osborne
- *For the City* by Matt Carter and Derrin Patrick
- *AND* by Hugh Halter and Matt Smay
- *It's Personal* by Brian Bloye and Amy Bloye
- *Transformation* by Bob Roberts Jr.
- *Missional Moves* by Rob Wegner and Jack Magruder

Available in stores and online!